*Measures of
Family Functioning
for Research and Practice*

Authors

Kathleen J. Sawin, DNS, RN, CS, FNP, is an Associate Professor and Co-Director, Weekend Family Nurse Practitioner Track, School of Nursing, Medical College of Virginia Campus, Virginia Commonwealth University. Her teaching focuses on primary care of families, children with chronic illness and disability, and research methods. Her research has focused on families with an adolescent who has a chronic illness or disability. Currently her practice is in the Spina Bifida Clinic at Children's Hospital, Richmond, Virginia, and in a migrant health project.

Marcia P. Harrigan, PhD, MSW, is an Associate Professor of Social Work at Virginia Commonwealth University, and Director of the MSW Program. She teaches social work practice and family behavior. Her research is focused on nontraditional families such as the multigenerational family household and foster family functioning. Her social work practice experience has been in child welfare (foster care and adoptions), juvenile corrections, and community mental health.

Editor

Pierre Woog, PhD, one of the founding editors of *Scholarly Inquiry for Nursing Practice,* is professor of Human Service Studies at Adelphi University as well as Professor of Education and Professor of Nursing. Formerly, he was the Founding Dean of Adelphi School of Education. He has extensive experience in graduate teaching and has consulted, authored articles and books, made presentations in the fields of Education, Nursing, Mental Health, Evaluation, Research Methodology, and Psychometrics, and has been an award-winning essayist for the journal *Evaluation and Health Professions.* He is also Editor of *The Chronic Illness Trajectory Framework* (Springer 1992), named Best Book of the Year in 1992 by the *American Journal of Nursing* and *Nurse Practitioner.*

Measures OF Family Functioning FOR Research AND Practice

Kathleen J. Sawin, DNS, RN, CS, FNP
Marcia P. Harrigan, PhD, MSW

Pierre Woog, PhD (EDITOR)

Springer Publishing Company

Springer Publishing Company, Inc.
536 Broadway
New York, NY 10012-3955

Cover design by Tom Yabut
Production Editor: Pamela Lankas

96 97 98 99 / 5 4 3

Library of Congress Cataloging-in-Publication Data

Sawin, Kathleen J.
   Measures of family functioning for research and practice /
Kathleen J. Sawin and Marcia P. Harrigan, authors;
Pierre Woog, editor.
      p. cm.
   Includes bibliographical references and index.
   ISBN 0-8261-8900-8
   1. Family—Research. 2. Family assessment.
3. Psychometrics.
   I. Harrigan, Marcia P. II. Woog, Pierre. III. Title.
HQ515.S29 1994
306.85'072—dc20   94-38528
                                                                CIP

Printed in the United States of America

Contents

Preface

Originally published as a special issue of the journal *Scholarly Inquiry for Nursing Practice,* the compendium you are about to peruse, read, and certainly go back to, is the best I have seen in my 25 years as a practitioner and teacher of psychometrics. It is incisive, comprehensive, intelligible, scholarly, and current. It can be read to locate and select the particular measure you really need, with all the background work done for you. It can be read as an overview of this area and its manifest problems. It can be read to convince you to create your own measure, knowing full well the task you have set before you.

Reading through the measures gives one a sense of chronicity. In the main, the movement from well-established to moderately established to developing measures is historical in nature. My reading from this perspective was done with a question in mind. The question was whether our construction of what a family is has changed over time. The instruments take us on a journey of 30+ years. Is the notion of family going through a reconstruction?

In obvious ways families have changed; they are more diverse, but the culture has changed as well. I think we can say that over time hope has diminished, and that fear of all kinds—fear of crime, fear of the other, fear of the environment, fear of economic viability—has escalated. Have these changed our construction of what family means? I think so. The earlier instruments concentrated on the family as an environment of growth, a kind of Petri dish of self-actualization. The current instruments have a dash of family as refuge, family as a relatively safe place, family as a corporation for financial survival. I don't think it is by chance that the *Assessment of Strategies in Families' Effectiveness* (1991) includes items such as, "Our neighborhood is bad and we have to protect ourselves from what's going on out there," and the *Comprehensive Evaluation of Family Functioning* (1990) has a subscale entitled "Financial." However, Sawin and Harrigan caution that "lack of theoretical consistency makes it difficult to compare data collected by different instruments. Researchers need to closely examine the items in the instrument to ascertain if they represent the concept they wish to study."

As we read through this compendium, the central postmodern truth, if I may use that term, becomes apparent. We, as curious, sense-making creatures, construct and reconstruct our realities. Our cultural artifacts, including our measures, must reflect our current societal constructions in order to have any validity.

PIERRE WOOG, PHD

Introduction

Nurses and other health professionals who work with families must make several decisions. What data from families will they collect? Are they interested in an individual's perception of the family or multiple perceptions? What conceptual underpinnings are important to working with families? Will they use self-report data, observational data, or a combination of both? Will they use an established qualitative instrument to assess family functioning or will a structured interview meet their needs? If they choose an instrument to assess family functioning, which instruments evaluate dimensions that are appropriate for nursing research and interventions? Which instruments can be used for clinical applications, research, or both?

The purpose of this Introduction is to present an overview and a critique of selected measures of family functioning available to the clinician and researcher. These include self-report instruments, a structured interview, and clinician rating scales. Because the family is a complex social system, numerous variables can be identified that explain family functioning. Having an array of options that operationalize family dynamics allows the researcher or clinician to select those measures most critical to the families of interest.

This work was undertaken because existing reviews of family instruments were found lacking in one or more of the following areas. Either they: (1) did not include the most recent family assessment instruments developed by nursing researchers (Berkey & Hanson, 1991; Bishop & Miller, 1988; Halvorsen, 1991; Touliatos, Perlmutter, & Strauss, 1990); (2) were not detailed enough to give researcher/clinician adequate information to choose a tool, such as providing examples of items (Berkey & Hanson, 1991; Bishop & Miller, 1988; Halvorsen, 1991); (3) did not supply information on cross-cultural usage or gender-sensitive issues, which was found to be true for all the included reviews; (4) did not report a synopsis of the major findings from nursing research using the instrument (Berkey & Hanson, 1991; Bishop & Miller, 1988; Grotevant & Carlson, 1989; Touliatos et al., 1990) or (5) were based on instrument information that was over 5 years old (Bishop & Miller, 1988; Touliatos et al., 1990; Halvorsen, 1991); and (6) did not reflect the family as the unit of analysis (Feetham, 1991a). If research questions focus on the family as the unit of analysis, as proposed by Feetham and others, information about readability level, length of questionnaire, and cost of instruments become even more important.

The development of these instruments is very dynamic. Although several "established instruments" are either undergoing major revisions (FACES III) or are being scrutinized for problems with psychometrics (FES), several new instruments (ASF-E, FFSS, and CEFF) are in initial stages of development, and several others are in the middle of their development (FDM, FHI, and FAM III). This analysis provides a critique of family functioning instruments in all stages of development. This will be helpful to both established researchers and novices seeking to choose or further develop an instrument appropriate for their needs. The clinician needs to carefully review information on clinical validation of potential instruments when considering using an instrument in the practice setting.

Understanding families demands an interdisciplinary sensitivity. As disciplines begin working together on programs of research with families, it is critical that they become familiar with the literature and measurements in each other's scholarly literature. As a result of such collaboration, concepts are clarified, assumptions are challenged, and new visions and applications are found. Thus, the measures addressed here reflect instruments from the disciplines of nursing, psychiatry, psychology, social work, and sociology. Although the interdisciplinary nature of the study of the family is recognized and supported, a concerted effort was made to include instruments generated and tested by nursing scholars. Included in this review are four such instruments: Feetham's Family Functioning Survey (FFFS); The Family Dynamics Measure (FDM); Family Hardiness Index (FHI); and Assessment of Strategies in Families (ASF-E). Three instruments representing the Beavers System Model used by many disciplines but seldom used in nursing research are also reviewed. These are included, as they provide a clinician rating approach to family investigation that is seldom used by nursing scholars.

Instrument Selection. For the selection of instruments in this critique, family functioning was defined as a set of basic attributes about the family system that characterize and explain how a family system typically appraises, operates, and/or behaves (McCubbin, 1987, 1991). For example, instruments that measured attributes such as family problem solving, hardiness, adaptability, individuation, and cohesion fit this criterion. Instruments that focused only on individual functioning, dyadic relationships, parent/child interaction, family stress, specific coping strategies, and social support were not reviewed. Instruments were identified from published literature. Computer searches of MEDLINE, CINAHL (Cumulative Index to Nursing and Allied Health Literature), and Psychological Abstracts for the last 5 years were carried out, and a manual search of Social Work Abstracts was done. Developers of the instruments were contacted for current materials including manuscripts in press. Drafts of critiques were sent to authors for response. Developers provided input for all instruments except in the category of early development, where the majority responded. When the author did not respond, the critique was based on published data.

Three categories of family functioning instruments were reviewed. Self-report instruments offer the opportunity to measure the perceptions of family members in a quantitative manner. Thus, they can be used to predict phenomena associated with family functioning. The other measures include observational and interview instruments, which offer several strengths. First, they organize qualitative data such as patterns of health or illness, the family within a social context, or family relationships across generations, and allow for family validation of data collected and classification of data. Second, they may offer a visual representation of individual and family system data and other variables influencing the family (for example, the relationship between subsystems within the family, and extended family relations). Finally, these instruments allow the uniqueness of a family to emerge from the data, as they are not limited totally by identified dimensions in a predetermined instrument. This allows the researcher/clinician to obtain data that explain the phenomenon of family functioning from the individual and family unit's perspective(s).

Fourteen of the instruments reviewed are self-report instruments. These were divided for this review into three groups: well established, moderately established, or newly established. Instruments were included as well established or moderately established self-report instruments if they had been used in published research other than instrument development studies in the period from January 1987 to June 1993. Studies with the main purpose of reporting reliability and validity data were classified as instrument development studies. Five instruments were classified as well established based on extensive psychometric evidence and wide use in the literature. Four instruments were classified as moderately established based on ongoing development of psychometric data and some use in the literature. Five instruments with psychometric data but with no or limited published use were classified as newly established.

Although this critique focuses on self-report instruments, the authors recognize the need to use multiple sources and methods to collect data. Instruments from the observational and interview categories give another perspective not obtainable in self-report inventories. Thus, four representative instruments are included in this review: a qualitative measure (genogram), a structured interview (McSIFF), and two clinician rating scales (Beavers Family Competence and Style Scales). Although other observational instruments exist, the Beavers scales were chosen, as the authors felt they were better developed with more psychometric evidence than other clinician rating scales reviewed (FAM Clinical Rating Scale, McMaster Clinical Rating Scale; and Clinical Rating Scale for the Circumplex Model of Marital and Family Systems [Grotevant & Carlson, 1989]).

Critique Format. Each review includes the following sections: History (of the instrument); Overview of the Model (including the conceptual framework); Instrument Description (including readability level if available, scoring options; sample items); Psychometric Properties (reliability and validity); a description of Cross-Cultural Uses, Gender Sensitivity, and Variant Family Structures; a Summary of Studies Using the Instrument; a Critique Summary; a Source to obtain the instrument and permission for use; and a table of Selected Studies Using the Instrument. User-friendly source information was included to optimize retrieval by the reader. Delineating the conceptual framework was deemed essential to understanding the instrument assumptions. Samples used, changes in the instrument over time, and a brief history of the instrument development are presented to orient the reader. Readability, scoring options, and sample items were included to facilitate the potential user's assessment of the match between the instrument and the population of interest. Psychometric data are critical to determine which instruments can be used with assurance of maximizing validity and reliability. Specifically, data on content, discriminant, predictive, concurrent, and construct validity, as well as internal reliability (Cronbach alpha), test–retest, and inter-rater reliability are presented. Studies reported in dissertations or theses were not included in the summary tables of studies using the instrument.

Particular attention in this analysis is paid to the different cultures the instrument has been used in and an examination of the validity and reliability in each of these cultures. Nurses work with a broad range of people representing various cultural, racial, and family types. Due to the increasing diversity in the general population, attention to reliability and validity of instruments measuring family functioning in diverse populations is critical. Researchers cannot assume that establishment of psychometric evidence in one population will apply to other populations.

Use of Family Functioning Instruments in Research and Practice. Consumers of instruments that measure family functioning are interested not only in the instrument itself, but in how it has functioned in studies that address variables of concern. The critique of the following instruments includes a review of the most recent studies pertinent to nursing practice that have used the instrument. Selected studies are presented in a tabular format for easy comparison. No tables are included for the newly established self-report instruments, the McSIFF, or for the Beavers Interactional Scales, as there is a limited body of supporting research in the literature using these instruments.

The critiques of the instruments are presented first. Following the 18 critiques, issues in the use of family functioning measures are discussed. This section includes an examination of measurement and analysis issues and the role of qualitative methods in family research. Finally, a concluding synthesis addresses implications of this review.

KJS
MH

1

Well-Established
Self-Report Instruments

THE McMASTER FAMILY
ASSESSMENT DEVICE (FAD)

History

The McMaster Model originated in the Departments of Psychiatry at McGill and McMaster Universities in Canada during the 1960s and 1970s under the initial direction of Nathan B. Epstein, MD. Based on research, teaching, and clinical work, its development continues at Brown University and Butler Hospital. The present research focuses on family functioning in families responding to physical and mental illnesses. Use of the Family Assessment Device which operationalizes the McMaster Model is occurring across a range of family types and problems found not only in the United States and Canada but worldwide. Research and clinical use has been both inter- and cross-disciplinary.

Overview of the Model

The McMaster Model is based on systems, role, and communications theories, and evolved from work with nonclinical families. An important theoretical assumption is that families can report healthy functioning in some dimensions while experiencing difficulties in other(s). The model is based on the assumption that, "The primary function of today's family unit appears to be that of a laboratory for the social, psychological, and biological development and maintenance of family members" (Epstein et al., 1976, p. 1411). In order to represent the complexities of a family, the model identifies six dimensions (structural and organizational properties) of family functioning: problem solving, communication, roles, affective involvement, affective responsiveness, and behavior control. Each dimension is operationally defined so that both optimal and pathological functioning is clear. Three assessment instruments have been developed based on this model. These are the Family Assessment Device (FAD), which is reviewed here, the McMaster Clinical

1

Rating Scale (MCRS) (Miller et al., in press), and the McMaster Structured
Interview for Family Functioning (McSIFF) also included in this review.

FAD INSTRUMENT DESCRIPTION

A 60-item self-report (paper and pencil) Family Assessment Device (FAD)
operationalizes the six family functioning dimensions. The general functioning scale (12 items) can be used independently from the other scales as
an over-all measure. A 4-point Likert-type scale is employed to determine a
member's perception of the family. The FAD has a seventh grade, or age 12,
readability level and takes approximately 15–20 minutes to complete.

Clinical cut points have been established to separate effective and potentially clinically problematic functioning families from each other. These
points can maximize sensitivity (proportion of actual "abnormal" results
accurately identified by the FAD) and specificity (proportion of actual
"normal" results correctly identified by the FAD) when compared to clinician ratings. Sensitivity ranged from .57 (Behavior Control) to .83 (Communication). Specificity ranged from .60 (Affective Involvement) to .79 (Problem Solving).

Scoring. The test includes both positive and negative statements that
require reverse scoring. Item responses then are totaled and averaged to
obtain a scale score. An easily applied tally sheet has been developed to
simplify hand scoring. Computerized scoring programs are also available
(see "Source" at end). Scores can be compared between family members or
a family score can be computed by averaging the scores for each member for
each scale.

The General Functioning Scale can be used as an overall measure of
family functioning. More specific identification of family strengths and
weaknesses is obtained by administering the entire instrument to obtain
measures of the six dimensions.

Sample Items. (dimension represented)

"We resolve most every day problems around the house"
(Problem Solving).
"When someone is upset the others know why" (Communication).
"When you ask someone to do something, you have to check that they did it"
(Roles).
"We are reluctant to show our affection for each other" (Affective Respon-
siveness).
"If someone is in trouble, the others become too involved" (Affective Involve-
ment).
"We know what to do in an emergency" (Behavior Control)

PSYCHOMETRIC PROPERTIES

Reliability

Internal Consistency. In the initial psychometric studies, coefficient alphas were the highest for the General Functioning Scale (.83–.86) and lowest for the Roles scale (.57–.69). For the remaining scales, the reliabilities were .74–.80 for Problem Solving; .70–.76 for Communication; .73–.75 for Affective Responsiveness; .70–.78 for Affective Involvement; and .71–.73 for Behavior Control (Epstein, Baldwin, & Bishop, 1983). Subsequent reports consistently support internal stability of all scales but the Roles scale (Harrigan, 1989; Joffe, Offord, & Boyle, 1988; Kabacoff, Miller, Bishop, Epstein, & Keitner, 1990; McKay, Murphy, Rivinus, & Maisto, 1991; Miller, Epstein, Bishop, & Keitner, 1985). In addition, the lowest reliabilities have been obtained for nonclinical samples, thus the Roles scale should be used very cautiously, particularly with nonclinical samples. Data using adolescent (Harrigan, 1989; McKay et al., 1991) and geriatric populations (Harrigan, 1989) yield comparable alphas.

Test–Retest. Reliability is based on data from a nonclinical sample of 45 individuals tested at a 1-week interval. The resultant test–retest estimates were Problem Solving (.66); Communication (.72); Roles (.75); Affective Responsiveness (.76); Affective Involvement (.67); Behavior Control (.73); and General Functioning (.71) (Miller et al., 1985). Similar test–retest data were reported by Browne, Arpin, Corey, Fitch, and Gafni (1990).

Inter-Rater Reliability. Not applicable.

Validity

Content Validity. The initial item pool for the FAD was developed from goal attainment scaling point descriptions from outcome studies. Additional items were added to cover all six dimensions, items were rewritten to ensure representation of only one dimension, and an equal number of healthy and unhealthy functioning items for each dimension was ensured. This resulted in 240 items, or six scales of 40 items each, in the first version of the FAD.

Construct Validity. Each 40-item scale was analyzed using Cronbach's alpha to result in the smallest subset of items that produced the highest reliability. At this point reliabilities ranged from .83 to .90, but the scales were highly intercorrelated. Selecting the items most highly intercorrelated resulted in the creation of a seventh General Functioning Scale, which continues to serve as an overall measure of health/pathology.

Three criteria then were applied to the 240 items: (1) the items had to be written for the relevant dimension; (2) the internal consistency had to reach at least .70 (alpha); and (3) each scale item had to correlate higher with the scale to which it was assigned than to any of the other six scales. Using a recursive method, the final scales were established when the minimal alpha level was reached while not increasing the magnitude of relationship of items with other scales. The item pool was reduced to 53 items comprising the first version of the FAD. Based on subsequent validity and reliability studies of clinical and nonclinical families, items were added to the Problem Solving (2), Communication (3), and Roles (3) scales respectively to complete the current version for the FAD (Epstein et al., 1983; Kabakoff et al., 1990). The most recent factor analysis used pooled data from nonclinical, psychiatric, and medical family samples (*n*=2,063). The Oblique Multiple Groups (OMG) factor analytic approach confirmed the internal structure of the six dimensions measured by the FAD. The General Functioning Scale (12 items) was omitted due to its designed correlation with the other scales. For the remaining 48 items, 44 (92%) loaded highest on the hypothesized factor. Based on two alternative factor models utilizing principal components analyses, the structure of the FAD (including the General Functioning Scale) corresponded adequately to the hypothesized (predicted) model (Kabacoff et al., 1990).

Concurrent Validity. The predicted relationships between the scales of the FAD and FACES-II, when treated linearly (Olson, Sprenkle, & Russell, 1979), and the FUI (Van der Veen & Olson, 1981; Van der Veen, Howard, & Austria, 1970) provided adequate evidence of concurrent validity for the FAD.

Regression analysis was used to test for concurrent validity of the FAD with the Philadelphia Geriatric Morale Scale (Lawton, 1972, 1975) and the Locke Wallace Marital Satisfaction Scale (Locke & Wallace, 1959). The results indicated that the FAD was a more powerful predictor than was the Locke Wallace for morale (Epstein et al., 1983).

Discriminant Validity[1]. Based on data from samples in which reporting members represented families that were clinically presenting (*n*=98) compared to individuals from families who did not present clinically (*n* = 218), 67% of the nonclinical group and 64% of the clinical group were correctly predicted by the FAD (Epstein et al., 1983; Miller et al., 1985; Perosa & Perosa, 1990; Sawyer, Sarris, Baghurst, Cross, & Kalucy, 1988; Waller, Calam, & Slade, 1989). On each of the seven scales, the nonclinical group mean was lower (more healthy) than the mean for the clinically presenting group (1983).

Predictive Validity. The FAD was found to be a better predictor of morale when compared to Locke Wallace Marital Satisfaction Scale data (Epstein et

---

[1]In this review, discriminant validity will refer to the ability of the measure to correlate negatively with other variables that are theoretically unrelated to the construct (Campbell & Fiske, 1959) or the ability of the measure to discriminate between criterion (known) groups (Hudson, 1982).

al., 1983). Family functioning also predicted the course of recovery for stroke victims (Evans, Halar, & Bishop, 1986). In more recent studies, functional/ dysfunctional families were significantly related to major depression recovery prognosis (Keitner, Ryan, Miller, & Norman, 1992; Miller et al., 1992). Greater degrees of dysfunction in affective responsiveness and role function- ing also were found to predict higher levels of substance abuse, particularly alcohol consumption (McKay et al., 1991). Finally, there is evidence that family functioning predicts psychiatric outcome in children (Maziade, Caperaa, & Laplante, 1985) and children's postdivorce adjustment (Portes, Howell, Brown, Eichenberger, & Mas, 1992).

General Scale. The majority of the studies cited above addressed only content and discriminant validity for the General Functioning Scale. However, other evidence offers support of predictive, concurrent, and construct validity of the General Scale (Byles, Byrne, Boyle, & Offord, 1988; Joffe et al., 1988; Kabacoff et al., 1990). This psychometric evidence provides ample support that this scale, composed of only 12 items, can serve as a valid and reliable measure of overall family functioning.

Other Data: Social Desirability. Correlations of the FAD with the Marlowe- Crowne Social Desirability Scale (Crowne & Marlowe, 1964) in a university sample of 164 individuals from 72 families were uniformly low. Correlations ranged from -.06 (Behavior Control) to -.19 (Affective Involvement) (Fristad, 1989). Corrections for Social Desirability with the FAD were not supported.

CROSS-CULTURAL USES, GENDER SENSITIVITY, AND VARIANT FAMILY STRUCTURES

Much of the psychometric evidence for the FAD was obtained from university samples that had adequate gender representation but were primarily white and middle socioeconomic level samples. Although not designed for use in cross- cultural studies, the FAD has been utilized in research with samples from several countries other than the U.S.A. and Canada based on the theoretical strength of the model (Morris, 1990). The FAD is available in English, French, Hungarian, Dutch, Portuguese, Spanish, and Afrikaans. Currently Russian, Chinese, Hebrew, Haitian, and Italian versions of the FAD are being prepared. These versions have been carefully translated and back-translated but valida- tion in the translated languages is not completed.

Although only one version of the FAD exists, it appears to be applicable (based on the strength of the model and the wording and content of items) to nontraditional family structures, such as single parent households and ex- tended family households (Harrigan, 1989). Cross-cultural family functioning comparison research has been done (Keitner et al., 1990). Research on perceptual differences of family functioning by gender is in process at the Family Research Program at Butler Hospital.

SUMMARY OF STUDIES USING THE FAD

Mental Health. The FAD (see Table 1.1) has been used with families responding to the demands of a wide range of psychiatric problems. These include alcohol dependence, depression, affective disorders, schizophrenia, adjustment, and bipolar disorders.

Families With Adolescents. The FAD has been used in clinical studies of families responding to adolescent suicide and other mental health issues.

Chronic Illness. The FAD has been used with families responding to the demands of a wide range of medical problems. These include systemic lupus, traumatic brain injury, stroke, rheumatoid arthritis, spinal cord injury, Parkinson's disease, and other disabilities.

CRITIQUE SUMMARY

The theoretical model for the FAD is perhaps one of the oldest and most researched (Westley & Epstein, 1969) family functioning projects. Its research credibility and clinical utility are evidenced by the multitude of applications of three measurement instruments and an intervention model with diverse populations. At least two other family functioning projects have credited the McMaster Model as the basis for their ongoing research (Lewis, Beavers, Gossett, & Phillips, 1976; Skinner, 1987).

Recent confirmation of the theoretical factor structure provides an even stronger rationale for the use of the FAD in family research (Kabacoff et al., 1990). Until the last few years, much of the research has been descriptive, with a heavy emphasis on comparison between clinical and nonclinical samples and establishment of clinical cut points. All scales except the Roles scale have demonstrated adequate reliability over time. Thus, users should either delete the Roles scale or interpret Role data with caution. A particular strength of the FAD is the number of languages in which the instrument is available, making it possible to study and compare families from a variety of cultures. The need for psychometric data to be established with different cultural populations is recognized and currently underway.

The McMaster Model of Family Functioning has been used to develop family assessment instruments other than the FAD for which the psychometric properties are presently being established. These are the McMaster Structured Interview of Family Functioning (McSIFF) included in this review and the

McMaster Clinical Rating Scale (MCRS). A problem-solving family intervention approach also has been developed (Bishop, 1981).

SOURCE

A current bibliography, FAD instrument packet, teaching videotapes, computerized scoring program, and other materials related to the McMaster Model are available by contacting Ivan W. Miller, Ph.D., Director of Research, Butler Hospital, 345 Blackstone Boulevard, Providence, RI 02906, or by calling 401-455-6200.

FAMILY ADAPTABILITY AND COHESION SCALE (FACES II, III, IV)

History

The Circumplex Model originated in the late seventies in the Family Social Science Program at the University of Minnesota under the direction of David H. Olson, Ph.D., and associates. The model is aimed at bridging the gap that frequently exists between practice, theory, and research. Several instruments to measure various dimensions of marital and family functioning have been developed, and research continues to increase support for their reliability, validity, and clinical utility. FACES II, III, and IV (under development) focus on the adaptability and cohesion dimensions of family functioning, as well as perceived and ideal family functioning.

Overview of the Model

Based on the identification of over 50 concepts related to family functioning from a systems perspective, three concepts are seen as the most central and descriptive of marital and family dynamics: cohesion, adaptability, and communication. These dimensions are seen as dynamic over the course of the family life cycle, with one family type being more functional at times than at others.

Cohesion describes the emotional bonding in a family, which can have four levels: disengaged (very low), separated (low to moderate), connected (moderate to high), and enmeshed (very high). Adaptability describes the ability of a family to alter its role relationships, power structure, and relationship rules in response to situational and developmental stress. Adaptability has four levels: rigid (very low), structured (low to moderate), flexible (moderate to high), and chaotic (very high). The most functional levels for both adaptability

Table 1.1. Selected Studies Using McMaster Family Assessment (FAD)

Author's citation	Variables	Samples/mMeasures	Major findings
Mental Health			
Keitner, Ryan, Miller, & Norman, 1992	Predictors of major depression recovery over 12-month period.	78 patients with DSM III-R diagnosis of major depression and their families. FAD (Total)	By 12th month, 48.6% met recovery criteria. Factors most related to recovery were: shorter length of hospital stay, older age of depression onset, better family functioning, less than 2 previous hospitalizations, absence of comorbid illness.
Keitner, Miller, Epstein, Bishop, & Fruzzetti, 1987	Major depression & family functioning	38 psychiatric inpatients with major depression and their families (28 control families) FAD (Total)	Families with depressed members had worse family functioning. Depression episode shorter in families that improved in family functioning during follow-up.
Keitner, Miller, Fruzzetti, Epstein, Bishop, & Norman, 1987	Depression, suicide, & family functioning	118 depressed patients with/without suicide behavior. FAD (Total)	Discrepancies on family functioning between subject and other family members correlated with suicide. Average family scores significantly lower with depressed members. NSD[a] found in average scores between family with suicide attempters or nonattempters. Suicide patients had least positive perception of family functioning.
Keitner, Fodor, Ryan, Miller, Bishop, & Epstein, 1991	Depression, culture, & family functioning.	62 Hungarians & 118 North Americans with DSM III-R diagnosis of major depression & 58 Hungarian and 95 North American control families.	Greater differences between North American groups on family functioning compared to Hungarian family groups. Problematic areas in family functioning differed by cultural group.

[a]NSD = no statistically significant difference

Study	Focus	Sample / Measure	Findings
Miller, Kabacoff, Keitner, Epstein, & Bishop, 1986	Psychiatric inpatients & family functioning	258 inpatients compared to 69 individuals from nonclinical sample FAD (Total)	Families of patients with major depression, alcohol dependence, and adjustment disorder had greater family dysfunction (mean scores). NSD[a] between families with schizophrenic members or those with bipolar disorder.
Miller, Keitner, Whisman, Ryan, Epstein, & Bishop, 1992	Family functioning and major depression: severity, chronicity, history, neuroendocrine functioning, & other psychiatric diagnoses.	68 patients with major depression and their families. FAD (Total)	Patients from dysfunctional families revealed significantly higher levels of neuroticism and poorer course of illness at 12-month follow-up.
Waller, Slade, & Calam, 1990a, 1990b	Anorexic & bulimic women's physical characteristics and perceptions of family functioning.	48 clinical (Anorexia & bulimia nervosa) and 30 comparison families. FAD (Total)	Perceptions of family functioning by patients were more accurate when compared to those of other family members in predicting family dysfunction.
Families With Adolescents			
Joffe, Offord, & Boyle, 1988	Suicidal behavior in children and adolescents & family functioning	Ontario Child Health Survey of 1,869 families General Functioning Scale	Family functioning (along with parent arrest, drinks, parents treated for "nerves," low income, and urban residence) was significantly related to suicidal behavior (either suicidal ideation or attempt).
Sawyer, Sarris, Baghurst, Cross, & Kalucy, 1988	Families with adolescents, individual perceptions, & family functioning	94 families with adolescents referred to mental health service and 94 community dwelling families with adolescents FAD (Total)	Members of clinic families rated families with lower family functioning. There was a significant difference between adolescents and their parents in both groups with adolescents rating family functioning lower.

[a]NSD = no statistically significant difference

(Continued)

Table 1.1. Selected Studies Using McMaster Family Assessment (FAD) *(Continued)*

Author's citation	Variables	Samples/mMeasures	Major findings
Chronic Illness Bishop, Epstein, Keitner, Miller, & Srinivasan, 1986	Chronic illness/disability & family functioning	Families with a member experiencing stroke FAD (Total)	Cognitive disturbances associated with poor family functioning. Family functioning associated with adjustment adherence to treatment, number of days in hospital. Education + counseling associated with smallest deterioration in FAD Scales after stroke.
Cunningham, Benness, & Siegel, 1988	Children with ADDH[b], time allocation, parental depression, & family functioning	Mothers/fathers in 52 two-parent families (26 ADDH[b], 26 control families) FAD (Total)	NSD[a] in family functioning in general and 6 specific subscales. Mothers were more depressed with higher alcohol consumption. Family functioning was related to depression in fathers and mothers.
Evans, Bishop, Matlock, Stranahan, & Noonan, 1987	The effect of selected stroke outcomes (i.e., dysphasia, Barthel index, liability perceptual neglect) on family functioning.	Caregivers of first-time stroke patient n = 78 FAD (Total)	Stroke outcomes were not related to family functioning.
Reeber, 1992	Family functioning/family education related to head-injured population	91 voluntary families in a 5-session education series focused on a head-injured member FAD	No statistically significant changes in mean scores before/after family education. Study did not control for severity of injury and other family interventions used.
Zarski, DePompei, & Zook, 1988	Traumatic head injury & family functioning	Parents or spouses of 45 head-injured patients FAD (Total) FACES III Family Invulnerability Test (FIT)	No significant correlation FAD & FIT Of family characteristics, only family satisfaction related to FAD. Five of the FAD scales and general scale significantly related to cohesion of FACES III (.30 & .66). Only 2 (problem solving & communication) correlated to FACES III adaptability scale.

[a]NSD = no statistically significant difference

and cohesion fall into the middle of the ranges and are labelled "balanced." Communication is viewed as the facilitating dimension for the other two. It is not included in the graphic model or measured separately by the FACES instruments.

When adaptability and cohesion are placed on horizontal and vertical axes to each other, 16 possible combinations emerge as possible types of families. This Circumplex model thus proposes a curvilinear relationship, with family functioning in the central ranges as the most functional and those on the extreme ranges the most dysfunctional. If all the family members are satisfied with extreme levels of functioning, however, the family can function well (Olson, 1989).

FACES INSTRUMENT DESCRIPTION

The FACES instrument is recommended as one of several needed to fully assess a family or marital system. Other instruments have been developed by the creators of the Circumplex model to obtain a clinician's perception (Clinical Rating Scale), which together with FACES II or III provides a multimethod approach. All three dimensions can be assessed (multitrait) using the Circumplex Assessment Package (CAP), which also measures family satisfaction. These instruments focus on assessment of the family as a whole, dyads, and other subsystems, resulting in a multisystem assessment. Family and couples versions are available.

There is considerable evidence that the present model must be operationalized as a linear measure when adaptability and cohesion scores are compared to numerous other measures of individual, dyadic, and family functioning with many populations (Green, 1989; Green, Harris, Forte, & Robinson, 1991a, 1991b; Hampson, Beavers, & Hulgus, 1988; Miller et al., 1985; Pratt & Hansen, 1987; Protinsky & Shilts, 1990). Several researchers, including Olson and associates, have discussed various options to modify FACES III in order to obtain theoretically and clinically sound results (Fristad, 1989; Green et al., 1991a, 1991b; Kuehl, Schumm, Russell, & Jurich, 1988; Olson, 1991; Perosa & Perosa, 1990a, 1990b).

Due to the identified measurement difficulties related to the curvilinear hypotheses, the Three Dimensional (3-D) Circumplex Model has been developed recently (Olson, 1991). This model theoretically incorporates second-order change (ability of a family to change to another type). The ability of a family to change itself (first-order change) has been a central assumption from the inception of the Circumplex Model. At this writing FACES IV is being tested by David Olson in collaboration with Robert G. Green and Volker Thomas (Green et al., 1991b; Olson, 1991). Until this new version is tested for validity and reliability, it is recommended that the 30-item FACES II be used with a revised scoring technique (Olson, Bell, & Portner, 1991). FACES II has demonstrated stronger psychometric properties over time when compared to FACES III.

Scoring. Thirty items comprise the instrument, with 16 Cohesion and 14 Adaptability items. A scale that ranges from 1 (almost never) to 5 (almost always) is used to record a person's perception of how frequently each item applies to one's own family. High scores on the Adaptability and Cohesion dimensions are reinterpreted as "very connected" and "very flexible" using the newly devised scale. A revised scoring technique for FACES III data has also been devised (Olson & Tiesel, 1991) and may be particularly useful for work in progress or reanalysis of existing data. Previously established cut points for both dimensions remain the same.

Mean scores that represent the family as a unit can be computed if individual scores are similar. If dissimilar, discrepancy scores provide a more accurate representation of the family unit. Both types of scoring allow for identifying the family type and identifying differing family perceptions. A detailed manual is available for easy scoring (Olson et al., 1991).

Sample Items. (dimension represented)

"Family members like to spend their free time with each other" (cohesion).
"It is difficult to get a rule changed in our family" (adaptability).

PSYCHOMETRIC PROPERTIES

Validity and reliability evidence for FACES IV is in the process of being established. Existing evidence for FACES II and III is presented here.

Reliability

Internal Consistency. Alpha reliability is higher for FACES II (.87 for Cohesion; .78 for Adaptability; .90 for total scale) due to the increased number of items when compared to FACES III (.77, .62, .68, respectively) (Olson et al., 1991).

Test–Retest Reliability. Over a period of 4 to 5 weeks, coefficients were .83 for cohesion and .80 for adaptability using FACES II based on a university and high-school sample of 124 students (Olson et al., 1991).

Inter–Rater Reliability. Not applicable.

Validity

Content Validity. Based on the clustering of 50 concepts identified by the developers which are used to describe marital and family dynamics, the three dimension of cohesion, adaptability, and communication were selected as central. No FACES measures attempt to measure communication, as other scales exist for this construct. FACES I was developed from 204 statements representing Cohesion (104) and Adaptability (100). The 204 statements were rated for clinical relevance by 35 marriage and family counselors and then administered to 410 young adults. Based on high content saturation assessed by counselor ratings, and a high factor loading established from data when administered, FACES I was created. It contained 54 Cohesion and 42 Adaptability items, and included the Edmonds Social Desirability Scale of 15 items.

Construct Validity. Using data from 201 families representing 603 respondents, factor analysis was applied and found to support the initial scales. FACES II was created to shorten the instrument, simplify the wording of items for use with children, decrease double negatives, and provide a revised 5-point response scale. Factor and reliability analyses of data from a sample of 464 adults reduced the instrument to 50 items. Based on data from a national sample of 1,140 couples and 412 adolescents representing the family life cycle stages (Olson et al., 1982, 1983) to which factor analysis was applied and reliability estimates computed, the 50 items were reduced to 30. Two formats were used to administer FACES II: perceived and ideal perceptions were obtained for which a discrepancy score was computed.

FACES III was developed to reduce the high correlation between Cohesion and Adaptability (down to .03) as well as social desirability. The 20 items that comprise this version were based on the same national sample as was FACES II (Olson, 1986, 1991).

Construct Validity. Factor analysis revealed evidence that the items load on the hypothesized factor. For Cohesion, loadings ranged from .34 to .61. For Adaptability, loadings ranged from .10 to .55 (Olson et al., 1991).

Concurrent Validity. Treating data obtained by FACES II in a linear manner has demonstrated some evidence of concurrent validity and is reported higher for FACES II than for FACES III (Hampson, Hulgus, & Beavers, 1991). Evidence is stronger for Cohesion and more equivocal for Adaptability (Beavers & Voeller, 1983; Green et al., 1991a, 1991b; Green, Kolevzon, & Vosler, 1985; Henggeler, Burr-Harris, Borduin, & McCallum, 1991; Olson, 1991; Pratt & Hansen, 1987; Walker, McLaughlin, & Greene, 1988).

Discriminant Validity. FACES III has discriminated between families presenting clinically and families with few difficulties and with respondents representing various problems (Edman, Cole, & Howard, 1990; Henggeler et al., 1991; Olson et al., 1991).

Predictive Validity. Better cohesion functioning as measured linearly by FACES III was found to predict better outcome in birth preparation classes (Langer, Czermak, & Ringler, 1990), less marital violence (Lehr & Fitzsimmons, 1991), and less adolescent substance abuse (Protinsky & Shilts, 1990).

Other Data. *Between-scale correlations* are higher for FACES II (r=.25 - .65) than for FACES III (r= .03). *Social desirability* evidence falls in the moderate range for FACES II (cohesion: r=.39; adaptability: r=.38) (Olson et al., 1991).

CROSS-CULTURAL USES, GENDER SENSITIVITY, AND VARIANT FAMILY STRUCTURES

The Three Dimension (3-D) Circumplex Model regarding extreme family types is purported to be less value biased, since within–family perceptions that are similar can be labelled extreme but viewed as functioning well. FACES II and III have been used with a broad range of family groups, including Mexican-Americans and Anglos (Flores & Sprenkle, 1988; Knight, Tein, Shell, & Roosa, 1992; Vega et al., 1986); lesbian and heterosexual couples (Zacks, Green, & Marrow, 1988); Austrians (Kirchler, 1988); Italians (Ardone & D'Atena, 1988); and Australians (Noller & Shum, 1990). Differences in family perceptions by gender have been found, such as female adolescents reporting more cohesion compared to males (Jackson, Dunham, & Kidwell, 1990).

SUMMARY OF STUDIES USING THE FACES

FACES II and III have been used with a broad range of problems addressed by nurses. These include eating disorders, substance abuse, chronic pain, child sexual abuse, perinatal outcomes, phenylketonuria, traumatic head injury, marital violence, coronary artery disease, and influenza. A summary of studies using FACES II and III is found in Table 1.2.

CRITIQUE SUMMARY

Literally hundreds of studies and family intervention programs that utilize the Circumplex Model and its measures provide strong evidence of its theoretical, research, and clinical applicability. The difficulties in measurement have yielded conflicting and confusing results. The revised scoring options for existing instruments and the current development of FACES IV using a bipolar scoring format look promising to address these problems.

The longer 30-item version of FACES II remains short in comparison to other instruments. It is easy to score and understand. The availability of several versions and broad applicability to a range of populations and problems result in a viable instrument for nursing research and clinical practice.

SOURCE

Instruments, scoring guides, manuals, bibliographies, and catalogs of all instruments are available from: Dr. David H. Olson, Ph.D., Family Inventories Project, Family Social Science, University of Minnesota, 290 McNeal Hall, St. Paul, MN 55108. Telephone: (612) 625-7250; FAX (612) 625-4227. The FACES II Manual is available for $30. The Family Inventories Manual is $65 and includes nine inventories in addition to FACES II.

FAMILY ENVIRONMENT SCALE (FES)

History

The Family Environment Scale, developed by Rudolf Moos and Bernice Moos in the 1970s, is one of the most used self-report measures of family functioning. It is one of a series of instruments on social climates. The initial choice and wording of the 200 items were the result of an interplay between data from interviews and observations of families and a conceptual formulation of three general domains (Moos, 1990). Developmental work (see content/face validity below) yielded the current 90-item true-false instrument. The original work reported in the manual (Moos, 1974; Moos & Moos, 1986) is based on a family sample of both normal ($n= 1,125$) and distressed ($n=500$) families (Moos & Moos, 1986). The instrument in this format has been used in over 300 studies. A shortened form of the instrument also has been developed (see other data below). Although the originators of the instrument report reliability and validity data, recent scholars have raised questions about the psychometric properties (Bloom, 1985; Loveland-Cherry, Youngblut, & Leidy, 1989; Munet-Vilaro & Egan, 1990; Roosa & Beals, 1990a, 1990b).

OVERVIEW OF THE MODEL

The FES assesses the social environment or climate of families from an interactionist framework. This framework presents behavior as an interaction of the person and the environment. The framework proposes that situational and environmental factors generate a substantial proportion of the variance in behavior (Skinner, 1987). The developers proposed that there are three domains that measure this climate or whole family functioning: social relationships among family members; personal growth; and family systems maintenance.

Table 1.2. Selected Studies Using Family Adaptation and Cohesion Evaluation Scales (FACES II & III)

Author's citation	Variables	Samples/measures	Major findings
Abell, Baker, Clover, & Ramsey, 1991	Birthweight, Adaptability & Cohesion, length of gestation	772 mother-infant pairs FACES II	12% of families unhealthy with extreme scores on Cohesion & Adaptability; significant relationship of poorer family functioning to lower birthweight controlling for other determinants
Benter, 1991	Perceived seriousness of child's illness, family crises, Adaptability & Cohesion	41 families FACES III	Findings did not consistently support the conceptual models
Clover, Abell, Becker, Crawford, & Ramsey, 1989	Influenza B infection, stress, family functioning	Two parents & child age 1-18 from clinic roster. Social Readjustment Rating Scale (SRRS), Family APGAR, FACES II	Family dysfunction on FACES II significantly associated with influenza B infection; no relationship of APGAR and SRRS to infection.
Coburn & Ganong, 1989	Bulimic behavior, family adaptability & cohesion	308 college women of which 20 were bulimic & 21 incipient. Bulimic Test FACES III	Significant relationship between bulimia and Cohesion; no significant relationship between bulimia and Adaptability.
Drory & Florian, 1991	Coronary artery disease, hardiness, behavior type, psychosocial adjustment, Cohesion and Adaptability	128 patients with diagnosis of coronary artery disease Hardiness Scale, Type A measure FACES III	Personality hardiness only significant correlate of adjustment.
Flores & Sprenkle, 1988	Family assessment of Mexican-Americans, family structure	959 Mexican-Americans compared to normative data FACES III	Modest relationship between acculturation & family structure but stronger & more consistent relationship of balanced scores with higher income.

Study	Focus	Sample / Measures	Findings
Friedman, Tomko, & Utada, 1991	Drug abusers, family therapy outcome, family characteristics	85 adolescent drug abusers and their mothers / Family Environment Scale (FES), Parent-Adolescent Communication Inventory (PACI), FACES III (total)	Better functioning on FES and PACI predicted better treatment outcome.
Henggeler, Burr-Harris, Borduin, & McCallum, 1991	Juvenile & young adult offenders & nonoffenders, Adaptability & Cohesion	Juvenile repeat and nonoffenders & young adult prisoners / FACES III	Evidence supported the curvilinear hypothesis for Cohesion, Adaptability & distance-from-center.
Kang, Kleinman, Todd, & Kemp, 1991	Cocaine abuse, individual & family functioning	95 adult cocaine users / Beck Depression Inventory, Hopkins Symptom Checklist-90, structured interview, FACES III	Positive linear relationship between individual & family Cohesion functioning; inconsistency with Adaptability.
Kawash & Kozeluk, 1990	Self-esteem & family type	327 8th graders / Coopersmith Self-Esteem Inventory (CSEI), Canadian Self-Esteem Inventory, FACES III	Using distance-from-the-center scores, moderate family scores related to the highest esteem.
Kirchler, 1988	Everyday experience & marital happiness	21 couples / FACES II	Happiness associated with frequency, positivity, perceptual accuracy, & effectiveness of spousal interaction & inversely related to conflict.
Langer, Czermak, & Ringler, 1990	Birth preparation, fetal outcomes, Adaptability & Cohesion	88 couples (70 controls) / FACES III	Tendency toward more functional family with group receiving birth education; no difference in fetal outcome or complications.
Lehr & Fitzsimmons, 1991	Marital violence, Adaptability & Cohesion	Husbands & wives from counseling agency / Conflict Tactic Scales & FACES III	Significant relationship between rigid Adaptability, disengaged Cohesion & marital violence.

(Continued)

Table 1.2. Selected Studies Using Family Adaptation and Cohesion Evaluation Scales (FACES II & III) *(Continued)*

Author's citation	Variables	Samples/measures	Major findings
Lundholm & Waters, 1991	Eating disorders and family types	190 university females Eating Disorders Inventory Disordered Eating & Weight Instrument, FACES III	Subjects with scores in extreme range with greater eating disordered behavior; distance-from-center linear score significantly related to 14 of 18 eating disorders measures.
Masselam, Marcus, & Stunkard, 1990	Communication, family functioning & school performance	40 families with adolescent in alternative school matched with 52 families with adolescent in public school Parent-Adolescent Communication Scale (PACS), FACES III	Significantly better balanced functioning and more positive communication in public school families; more congruence between perceived & ideal family functioning in public school families.
Mathis & Tanner, 1991	Life stage & family functioning	47 couples, aged 51–79 years compared to Olson's national data for 4,509 adults; FACES III, Family Satisfaction Scale	Later-life couple satisfaction significantly higher, with Adaptability scores in unhealthy range; no differences on Cohesion between groups.
Mathis & Yingling, 1990	Marital status & family functioning	85 couples in divorce mediation; FACES III	Significantly lower Cohesion of divorcing couples compared to normative data; no difference on Adaptability.
McLinden, 1990	Special needs children & social support, impact, family satisfaction and functioning	48 mothers & 35 fathers FACES III, Comprehensive Evaluation of Family Functioning Scale (CEFF)	30% of mothers &/or fathers reported problems with support, satisfaction, & impact; significant differences between parents' responses for CEFF time demands, coping, and well-being.
Mengel, Blackett, Lawler, Volk, Viviana, Stamps, Dees, Davis, & Lovallo, 1992	Family functioning, diabetic control, stress response, & adherence behavior	Pilot of 12 adolescents, ages 15–18, with IDDM more than one but less than 10 years, and two parental figures without IDDM in household; FACES III, Schlenk & Hart self-report & observational questionnaire, glycosylated hemoglobin level, Kveback Family Sculpture Technique, Diabetes Family Behavioral Checklist, Inventory of Family Feelings, videogame with subsequent measures of pulse, blood pressure, epinephrine, norepinephrine, & glucose	Bivariate analyses revealed more diabetic control related to: more adolescent-perceived Cohesion; less discrepancy between real/ideal adolescent-mother dyad; less perceived dysfunction by mother and father; more father-perceived distance between real/ideal adolescent-father dyad; more positive maternal feelings toward adolescent; less adolescent-perceived nonsupportive mother behavior; and less mother-perceived problems with adolescent.

Study	Variables	Sample & Instruments	Findings
Novy, Gaa, Frankiewicz, Liverman, & Amerikaner, 1992	Juvenile offenders, ego development, Cohesion and Adaptability	61 nonchronic juvenile offenders and their parents (4 post hoc comparisons) Washington University Sentence Completion Test, FACES III	Lower levels of ego development significantly related to: (a) shared dysfunctional family perspective of juveniles & parents, and (b) juvenile functional perspective not shared with either parent.
Patton & Noller, 1991	Adolescent unemployment & family functioning	216 adolescents from 3 metropolitan high schools in Australia and their parents Socioeconomic Level Scale (SEL), FACES III	Two-year study resulted in significantly less Cohesion reported by unemployed adolescents & parents at T1-3; parents of both adolescent groups, unemployed males & females, and employed males wanted more Cohesion.
Philichi, 1989	Child hospitalization, Adaptability, Cohesion & coping	30 families with child in pediatric intensive care FACES III F-COPES	Families reported balanced family health and used variety of coping mechanisms.
Piercy, Volk, Trepper, & Sprenkle, 1991	Drug use characteristics, family structure and dynamics	151 drug-using adolescents Parent Adolescent Communication Inventory (PACI) FACES III	Cohesion, discipline, & open communication with mother more salient than family structural factors in discriminating drug use, patterns.
Primomo, Yates, & Woods, 1990	Social support, depression, illness demands, marital quality, family functioning	125 chronically ill women Norbeck Social Support Questionnaire, CES-D, Dyadic Adjustment Questionnaire, FACES II	Most perceived support from partner followed by health care providers, counselors, or religious personnel; affect, affirmation, & reciprocity associated with less depression, higher marital quality, & better family functioning.
Protinsky & Shilts, 1990	Substance & cohesion	237 7th & 8th grade students FACES III	Linear relationship with substance-abusing adolescents reporting disengaged families.

(Continued)

19

Table 1.2. Selected Studies Using Family Adaptation and Cohesion Evaluation Scales (FACES II & III) *(Continued)*

Author's citation	Variables	Samples/measures	Major findings
Richards, 1989	Differentiation, marital compatibility, Adaptability & Cohesion	60 volunteer married couples Level of Differentiation of Self Scale (LDSS), Locke-Wallace Marital Adjustment Scale (MAT), FACES III	Significant canonical relationship among differentiation, marital compatibility & Cohesion for wives only.
Roy & Thomas, 1989	Chronic pain & marital relations	52 chronic pain patients & their spouses Couple Version FACES III	Reported difficulties by couples in most all dimensions of Adaptability & Cohesion; more Adaptability discord; significant agreement between spouses; mid to extreme range.
Sawin & Marshall, 1992	Developmental outcomes of adolescents with spinal cord injury, family functioning, coping, autonomy, decision making, hope	Convenient sample of 32 adolescents with spinal cord injury. Harter's Self Perception Profile, Adolescent Psychosocial Functional Assessment Tool, Snyder's hope, protectiveness, FACES III, McCubbins ACOPE	Family functioning predicted only 1 domain specific developmental competence. Both teens' Cohesion ($r=.44$) & Adaptability ($r=.39$) scores but not family APGAR scores were related to behavioral conduct subscales (Harter). Teens who perceived their families as cohesive & adaptable were more likely to have positive perception of their own behavior.
Shulman, Fisch, Zempel, Gadish, & Chang, 1991	Functioning of families & children with phenylketonuria	43 families & children phenylalanine level, WISC-R; Adherence to Diet; Reiss Card-Sort Problem Solving Procedure; FAM III; F-COPES; The Child Behavior Checklist (CBCL)	Significant positive relationships among perceived Cohesion, dietary adherence; child IQ; paternal perception of Adaptability significantly related to IQ; child depression as perceived by parents related to family functioning and coping.
Trepper & Sprenkle, 1988	Child sexual abuse & family functioning	Sexually abused children & families in treatment. FACES III	Most families reported functioning that fell into extreme quadrant patterns; case example provided to show Circumplex model use for assessment & treatment.

Study	Topic	Sample & Measures	Findings
Vega et al., 1986	Ethnic group differences in family functioning	147 Anglo and 147 Mexican-American parents of school-age children	No significant difference in family functioning by ethnic group.
Walker, McLaughlin, & Greene, 1988	Somatization & family functioning	123 outpatients and their mothers FACES II, heath opinion survey, self-esteem inventory	Findings did not support curvilinear hypotheses for Cohesion or Adaptability; questioned construct validity of Cohesion & Adaptability as measured by FACES & compared to clinical assessments.
Waller, Slade, & Calam, 1990a, 1990b	Eating disorders and family functioning	47 women with eating disorder and 27 controls; Eating Attitudes Test (EAT) FACES II	Eating disordered women with lower Adaptability & Cohesion; no linear relationship between EAT scores & family functioning.
Woods, Haberman, & Packard, 1993	Family functioning, demands of illness, family adaption	125 women in Family Impact Study Demands of Illness - DOILL (and 7 subscales); Individual Adaption, CES-D Depression scale, FACES III, FAPGAR, DAS (Dyadic Adaption Scale)	FACES and APGAR both are associated with the family functioning subscale of DOILL ($r = .32$ and .39). APGAR had low but significant relationships with personal demands (body image $r = .16$ and personal meaning -.29). Women with more demands directly related to illness had more depression. Women who deal with persistent symptoms may be most at risk for negative outcomes.
Zacks, Green, & Marrow, 1988	Sexual orientation & family functioning	52 lesbian and normed data for 1,140 heterosexual couples FACES III & Family Satisfaction Scale	Lesbians reported significantly higher Cohesion, Adaptability, and satisfaction compared to heterosexuals.
Zarski, DePompei, & Zook, 1988	Traumatic head injury and family functioning	Parents or spouses of 45 head-injured patients FAD (total), Family Invulnerability Test (FIT), FACES III	Of family characteristics, only family satisfaction related to FAD; 6 of FAD scales significantly related to Cohesion of FACES III; only 2 FAD scales correlated with Adaptability.

FES INSTRUMENT DESCRIPTION

This 90-item self-report questionnaire has 10 subscales in the three conceptual domains:

1. The social relationship domain consists of the subscales Cohesion, Expressiveness, and Conflict:

(a) Cohesion: The degree of commitment, help, and support family members provide for one another.
(b) Expressiveness: The extent to which family members are encouraged to act openly and to express their feelings directly.
(c) Conflict: The amount of openly expressed anger, aggression, and conflict among family members.

2. The personal growth domain includes independence, achievement orientation, intellectual-cultural, active recreational orientation, and moral religious emphasis:

(a) Independence: The extent to which family members are assertive, are self-sufficient, and make their own decisions.
(b) Achievement Orientation: The extent to which activities (such as school and work) are cast into an achievement-oriented or competitive framework.
(c) Intellectual-Cultural Orientation: The degree of interest in political, social, intellectual, and cultural activities.
(d) Active Recreational Orientation: The extent of participation in social and recreational activities.
(e) Moral-Religious Emphasis: The degree of emphasis on ethical and religious issues and values.

3. The family system maintenance includes organization and control:

(a) Organization: The degree of importance of clear organization and structure in planning family activities and responsibilities.
(b) Control: The extent to which set rules and procedures are used to run family life.

Three forms of the FES are available: real (R), idealized (I), and expected (E). Respondents are instructed to indicate whether the item is true of their families from their perspective. If they feel that some of the statements are true for some family members and false for others, they are to mark 'true' if the statement is true for most members. Administration time is 20–40 minutes. Reading level: age 12. A child version exists (see other data below).

Scoring. The manual (Moos & Moos, 1986) reports a scoring protocol and comes with a scoring template. Family scores are averages of individual scores. In addition, either individual or family scores can be converted into standard scores. A protocol for calculating a family incongruence score measuring the extent of disagreement among family members is also given.

Norms for both normal and distressed populations, regular and stan
were developed from a study of 1,125 normal and 500 distressed
recent study (Wilk, 1991), however, questions whether the norms p
the manual have become outdated due to societal changes. In a study of 112
distressed family members (families that had a chronically mentally ill adult),
the mean values of FES scales were consistently higher than those of distressed
families from the original sample. Wilk's families bore a stronger resemblance
to the normal than the distressed families in the original study. Wilks cites
societal changes in attitudes toward mental health treatment and self-help
groups as influences that may have altered the 'norms' for the distressed
families and cautions researchers to be judicious in any comparison. However,
Moos counters that families with a chronically mentally ill adult may not be
distressed and may have adapted well to the chronic problem.

It is possible to develop a summed score called the Family Relationship
Index. This 27-item index is composed of the FES Cohesion, Expressiveness,
and Conflict scales and has been used as an overall measure of family support.
An additional scoring option to obtain a classification of family typology is
also available. Classification rules allow for identification of seven family
types. Classification by type allows for study of typology characteristics and
perhaps creates ideas from which to generate interventions. Ninety percent of
families in the classification study were assigned to a type according to the
classification rules generated.

Sample Items. (Dimension represented)

Family members really help and support one another (Cohesion)
Family members often keep their feelings to themselves (Expressiveness)
We fight a lot in our family (Conflict)
There is very little privacy in our family (Independence)
Family members share strict ideas about what is right and wrong (Control)
Family members rarely worry about job promotions, school, grades, etc.
(Achievement Orientation)

PSYCHOMETRIC PROPERTIES

Initial psychometric studies supported both the validity and reliability of the
instrument (Moos & Moos, 1986). Recently, however, both the proposed three-
domains structure and the reliability of select scales have been questioned.

Reliability

Internal Consistency. Internal consistency data from original sample range
from .61 for Independence to .78 for Cohesion, Intellectual-cultural orientation, and Moral-Religious Emphasis subscales (Moos, 1974). Recently, there

has been a spirited challenge to the reliability of several of the FES scales (Horton & Retzlaff, 1991; Loveland-Cherry et al., 1989; Munet-Vilaro & Egan, 1990; Roosa & Beals, 1990a, 1990b; Stuifbergen, 1990). Roosa and Beals found that five subscales (Cohesion, Expression, Conflict, Organization, and Control) had unacceptable reliabilities in one or more of their samples (families dealing with alcohol, asthma, bereavement, divorce, and control families). Loveland-Cherry et al. found reliabilities ranging from .13 for Independence to .80 for Moral-religious. Stuifbergen (1990), Margalit (1990), and Horton and Retzlaff (1991) report unacceptable reliabilities for independence. In addition Loveland-Cherry et al. found widely varying reliabilities for the children in the sample. It appears that the true-false format causes indecision and difficulty with interpretation and may account for the low reliabilities (thus high measurement error). In addition, Munet-Vilaro and Egan (1990) found that several translations of the FES (Puerto Rican and Vietnamese) had consistently low reliabilities (see cultural section).

Moos (1990) responds to the challenge of low internal reliabilities by indicating that the psychometric characteristics of a scale should not be "cross-validated" on a narrow sample with restricted item or subscale variability. He cautions researchers not to overlook validity in an unrealistic pursuit of reliability. He also acknowledges that the Independence scale sometimes shows relatively low consistency and that a multiple-choice response pattern may increase reliabilities. Roosa and Beals, however, report that low reliabilities make interpretation of scores difficult and attenuate relationships with other variables. They recommend that all authors report reliabilities with each population under study (1990a, 1990b).

Test–Retest Reliability. Eight-week test-retest reliabilities varied from .73 to .86; 12-month stabilities for averaged family subscale means varied from .63 for Cohesion to .81 for Organization. Select scales were examined for test-retest reliability at 36- and 48-month intervals. Test-retest at 36 months was .59 for Cohesion and .67 for Conflict and Control. The 48-month test-retest values varied from .45 to .54. Moos (1990) concluded that FES subscale scores may be quite stable over intervals of as long as 4 years.

Inter-Rater Reliability. Not applicable.

Validity

Content Validity. The final 90 items were selected according to the following criteria: (1) variability in item response frequency; (2) highest correlation with own subscale; (3) evenly split true/false-keyed items on each scale; (4) low to moderate scale intercorrelations; and (5) discrimination among families.

Construct Validity. In the initial studies of the instrument, the average item-scale correlations ranged from .27 for independence to .44 for cohesion. The manual does not provide specific data on item analysis or fact (Moos, 1974; Moos & Moos, 1986).

Subsequent analysis evaluated a large heterogenous sample of ¡ (*n*=992) (Oliver, Handal, Enos, & May, 1988). First, items were analyzed and 8 (rather than 10) scales were obtained with correlations between the original scales and the newly proposed scales ranging from .54 to .88. No parallel scale for Expressiveness was identified. The second study used factor analyses on scale scores to see if the proposed dimensions could be supported. A two-rather than three-factor structure was supported, with cohesion versus conflict and organization-control factors emerging. This study supported several others that identified two dimensions using either maximum likelihood factor structure or canonical analysis (Fowler, 1981, 1982).

Another recent factor analysis of scale scores (Kronenberger & Thompson, 1990) yielded differing factor structures depending on the sample. The first factor study of 88 caregivers identified three factors. The first factor had high loadings for Cohesiveness, Expressiveness, and two growth scales (named Supportive). Conflict and Organization loaded heavily on the second Conflict factor and Control, Moral-religious, and Independence (negatively) on the factor identified as Control. The Relationship factor of the original FES correlated with the Supportive factor *r*=.75.

The second study (*n* = 1,468 adults and 621 adolescents) replicated with minor changes the three-factor solution (Supportive, Controlling, Conflicted). The Supportive factor measures family mutual interest, concern, and support across a wide domain. The Conflicted factor reflects conflict and lack of organization. The controlling factor represents the use of competition and rules to control the family and foster a lack of independence. This three-factor solution accounts for substantially more of the variance (over 50% vs. 34%; 29% and 30%, respectively, for data cited above), is reproducible to families without chronically ill children, and allows for data reduction into three broad categories which can facilitate clinical research.

Other researchers have also tried to develop factor type or clusters. Stuifbergen (1990), using a cluster analysis, identified four clusters from mean standard scores: Cohesive cluster, Moral/religious cluster, Structured Conflict cluster, and Unstructured Conflict cluster. The scales named were the dominant scales in the cluster. Families differed on symptoms (Sickness Impact Profile) varying by cluster.

Moos (1990) argues that even though it is reasonable to try to identify a consistent set of constructs to characterize a family social environment, there are serious problems looking for the "factor structure." He proposes that the factor analysis will depend on the sample used, with more factors likely to emerge in more heterogeneous samples. In addition, the author proposes that due to the complexity of the family, the subscale level data reflect meaningful family characteristics that cannot be captured by large two or three domain factors. This author proposes that conceptual domains and patterns are more meaningful than factor or cluster analysis (R. Moos, personal communication, January 1994).

Concurrent Validity. FES subscales have been associated with a variety of life stressors including: adaptation to childhood illness, adjustment among families of psychiatric and medical patients, adaptation to pregnancy and parenthood, child's and adolescent's adjustment to divorce, the outcome of treatment for depression, and the outcome of treatment for alcoholism (Moos & Moos, 1986). Further, the Cohesion scale of the FES was correlated .86 with the FACES III Cohesion, .68 with the Affective Involvement scale of the FAD, and from .64 to .89 of the Cohesion-like scales for the Structured Family Interaction Scale-Revised (Perosa & Perosa, 1990).

Predictive Validity. A variety of studies including the impact of divorce on childhood and adolescent adjustment, the impact of family environment on infant temperament, predicting treatment outcomes in psychiatric and medical group, and predicting attrition from treatment are reported in the manual (1986). The scales measuring Cohesion, Expressiveness, Conflict, Independence, Recreational, and Religious are the most frequently found to be predictors.

Discriminant Validity. Moos and Moos (1986) report numerous studies in which FES subscales discriminate between families with a specific characteristic (abusive families, families with a delinquent, families in psychotherapy, families of substance abusers) and normal families. The at-risk families have somewhat differing patterns by problem; however, many of the distressed families were low on Cohesion, Expressiveness, Organization, Intellectual Orientation, and Recreational Orientation, and high on Conflict.

Other Data. Alternative form #1. A 50-item (5 items in each of 10 subscales) FES scale was identified using cluster analysis by Bloom in 1985. This study (269 college students) used a 4-choice format (very untrue for my family, fairly untrue for my family, fairly true for my family, very true for my family) rather than the original 2-choice (true-false), as the 2-choice format was not felt suitable for factor analytic cluster analysis, which depends on stable zero-order correlation coefficients. This shortened version and the long version had a comparable factor structure (all items on 50-item scale were also on 90-item scale) and reliability patterns (with only Independence and Achievement-orientation being below .64) and had a high interscale correlation (.90 and above) for parallel scales with acceptable reliabilities (Independence and Achievement of .84 and .86 with the parallel long-version scales). In addition, interitem correlations were consistently higher on the shortened scales. The author proposed that the shorter scales were more homogenous. In addition, Bloom (1985) concluded that the shortened scales appeared to be as sound psychometrically as the longer version but indicated that the scales of Independence and Achievement were not sufficiently reliable to be used with confidence. The author also indicated that the five items on the Moral-religious scale had religious specific content rather than moral content. Bloom (1985) used this shortened form of the FES as the basis for a new multi-tool factor structure, The Family Functioning Scale (see page 78).

The other "form" of the FES is reported in the manual: the Children's Family Environment Scale, a 30-item pictorial adaptation for children 5 to 11. The Children's FES Manual provides extensive normative and psychometric information (Moos & Moos, 1986). Little use of the instrument has been reported in family research in health settings, however.

CROSS-CULTURAL USES, GENDER SENSITIVITY, AND VARIANT FAMILY STRUCTURES

Early data included a combined middle-class minority sample (178 Mexican-Americans and blacks) but no normative data or psychometrics were provided on these data (Moos, 1974). Only nonsignificant slight differences were found between this minority sample and others in the normative study. The relationship between family functioning and behavior problems with a Mexican-American population was investigated by Martinez, Hays, and Soloway (1979) and the impact of disability on family functioning by Arnold and Orozco (1989). The latter study found differences between study population and normative sample on 9 of the 10 scales (not control). Neither study, however, reported any reliability or validity data with the minority samples.

The short form has been adapted to Hebrew and showed internal consistencies of .62 to .89 (Margalit, Leyser, Abraham, & Levy-Osin, 1988) and FES was used in subsequent analysis. No gender differences were found, but two FES domains, relationship and personal growth, which are typically female concerns, added significantly to the multiple regression prediction of sense of coherence scores.

Early use of the FES yielded general comparability to the English version in Dutch, French, and German (Moos & Moos, 1986). However, more recently when the FES has been translated into Puerto Rican and Vietnamese, the reliabilities have been consistently low (Munet-Vilaro & Egan, 1990). The standard "back translation" method was used in translations of the instruments. The authors propose that the literalness of the translation might be a deficit rather than an asset. Both of these cultures are very different from the American population in which the instrument norms were established. For example, in the Expressiveness scale the item "We tell each other about our personal problems" might not be appropriate for a Hispanic or Vietnamese subject. The cross-cultural athletic activities are also not equivalent. In addition, the negatively worded questions are not common in these languages and might yield erroneous responses. The basic issue may be that the environment of families may change significantly across cultures. The items' intent rather than content may need to be translated. It may be important that concept equivalency and concept differences be established before attempting to measure a concept in a culturally diverse population.

SUMMARY OF STUDIES USING THE FES

The studies using the FES as a measure of family functioning in the last 7 years generally fit into two categories: those comparing family functioning norms in an at-risk population and those using the FES scales to predict an outcome. In the studies summarized on the attached table (Table 1.3), outcomes such as depression, behavioral problems, adjustment, metabolic control of diabetes, adherence to treatment regimen, and social competence are explored. The scales most frequently predictive of these outcomes are Conflict and Cohesion. Families with higher Cohesion and lower Control tend to have better outcomes.

CRITIQUE SUMMARY

The FES is one of the oldest family functioning self-report instruments and has been widely used. The 90-item instrument has a fairly stable 8 to 10 subscale pattern. The three major dimensions proposed by the authors (Relationship, Growth, and Systems Maintenance), however, have not been supported by other factor analyses. Both a two-factor (Cohesion-conflict and Organization/control) and a three-factor structure (Support, control, conflict) have been reproduced by slightly different methods. The higher-order factors identified in these studies represent both a conceptual and methodological contribution to the study of family's role in a variety of outcomes. If researchers are going to collapse individual scales into factors for further analysis, use of one of these schemata rather than the originally proposed dimensions would have merit.

The instrument is easily administered in the clinical or research setting although it may take 20–40 minutes to complete. Forms exist to obtain discrepancy scores (real-ideal). A shortened 5-item version of the scales appears to be useful for both research and practice (Bloom, 1985; Loveland-Cherry et al., 1989). Cohesion, Conflict, Control, and Moral-religious seem to be essential subscales with some proposing Cohesion as the integrating concept throughout the scale (Bloom, 1985). It is one of the few instruments with a version useful in children under the age of 11. If one of a researcher's main concepts of interest is independence, this instrument may not be optimal due to consistent low reliabilities. In addition, Expressiveness and Achievement orientation subscales had questionable reliabilities across studies (Bloom,

1985; Loveland-Cherry et al., 1989; Moos, 1990). The true–false format may be a deficit for instrument reliability, and investigators may want to consider a 4-choice format (Bloom, 1985). Further studies may be needed to validate normative scores for distressed populations.

SOURCE

Consulting Psychologists Press, Inc., 3803 E. Bayshore Road, Palo Alto, CA, 94303. Telephone: (415) 969-8901 or (800) 624-1763; FAX (415) 969-8608. Materials can be obtained upon completion of a qualifying form. An annotated bibliography is available from Dr. Moos at the Center for Health Care Evaluation, Stanford University (415) 858-3996.

Table 1.3. Selected Studies Using Family Environment Scale (FES)

Author's citation	Variables	Samples/measures	Major findings
Arnold & Orozco, 1989	Physical disability acculturation family functioning	38 bilingual Mexican-American subjects who had a family member with a disability and in a State Vocational Rehabilitation caseload. Acculturation Rating Scale for Mexican-Americans; FES	Scores on 9 of the 10 subscales differ significantly from normative data. The moral-religious emphasis in these families may have framed their view of disability. Families of bilingual bicultural Mexican-Americans who encourage expression of emotions and are assertive help their family member progress to their vocational outcome.
Breslau, 1990	Children with physical condition involving brain dysfunction; environmental stress psychological symptoms, mother's depression	157 children with cerebral palsy, spina bifida, or multiple handicaps, and their mothers; 339 randomly selected controls; cross-sectional design Interviews (including NIMH-Diagnostic Interview Schedule for Children), FES, CDC depression scale for mothers	In multiple regression analysis, Cohesion (FES) predicted children's self-reported depression symptoms after controlling for age, sex, and IQ of child. Findings of this study provided no support for the hypothesis that brain dysfunction renders children vulnerable to environmental stress.
Brinson, 1991	Gender, alcohol use, family functioning	Black adolescents (12-20) (35 females and 36 males) from medical facility which provides outpatient substance abuse services. Interview including Alcohol and Drug Screening Questionnaire; Self-report: Drug Exposure Response Sheet and FES. Regular users = drank at least once a week and used medium amount per use.	Results suggest that females have a more favorable perception of family function in four areas. The female users perceived their family environments as more expressive and perceived more organization than male users; also perceived more emphasis on Independence and on Moral-religious issues.

Study	Variables	Sample/Measures	Findings
Dyson, Edgar, & Crnic, 1989	Psychological predictors; adjustment by siblings of developmentally disabled children	55 older siblings of disabled children and 55 older siblings of nondisabled children. Child Behavior Checklist; Piers Harris Self-Concept Scale; FES, Family Support Scale; Questionnaire on Resources and Stress.	Psychological factors accounted for 17% of the variance in behavior problems (Relationship dimension with scales of Cohesion, Expressiveness, and Conflict contributing); 40% of the variance in social competence of siblings with disabilities was predicted, with the personal growth dimension of FES contributing 32% variance (Independence, Moral-religious, and cultural-recreational activities). In homes where these domains were emphasized, the siblings were more socially competent. Children without siblings with disabilities had slightly different predictive patterns.
Fife, Huhman, & Keck, 1986	Stress, coping, family functioning; anxiety, marital adjustment, psychological functioning	34 patients, 33 mothers, 27 fathers, & 31 siblings of newly diagnosed leukemia followed by 1 year from time of diagnosis. Locke-Wallace Marital adjustment; Spielberger State-trait; MMPI FES; In-depth qualitative interviews for 10 families (5 with effective functional systems; 5 ineffective); school data	Measure of coping and functioning reflected fairly consistent patterns over the year. Families with stable relationships and support were able to cope with the stress of diagnosis and treatment. Families with existing problems at diagnosis had the most negative outcomes.
Hauser et al., 1990	Adherence; family functioning	52 teens/preteens newly diagnosed with diabetes and parents. 43 two-parent and 9 one-parent families followed for 4 years. Professional adherence index (multiple data over 4 years) and FES (annually).	Adherence decreased over the years. Family conflict as experienced by the teen is the strongest predictor of short- and long-term adherence. Parental cohesion also related to long-term adherence.

(Continued)

31

Table 1.3. Selected Studies Using Family Environment Scale (FES) *(Continued)*

Author's citation	Variables	Samples/measures	Major findings
Kronenberger & Thompson, 1990	Childhood behavior family functioning	109 chronically ill children and a parent Missouri Children's Behavior checklist. FES.	Factor analysis of scale scores yielded three higher-level dimensions: Supportive, Conflict, and Control. Children with behavior problems had families characterized as less supportive and more conflicted than those without behavior problems.
Kronenberger & Thompson, 1992	Family functioning, social coping; couple relationship; psychological distress	68 mothers of children with spina bifida Medical Indices scale; FES; Dyadic Adjustment Scale (DAS); Social Adjustment Questionnaire (SAQ); Social Coping Questionnaire (SCL); SCL–90 including Global severity Index (GBI)	Somatization, Depression Anxiety and GSI scales significantly above norms; 44% of sample had poor psychological adjustment. Predictors of poor psychological distress: Marital quality and controlling family environment doubled R^2 from demographic variables only (total R^2=.50). Less controlling family environment related to better adjustment. Coping NS related to psychological distress.
Margalit, 1990	Gender, social skills, personality family functioning	742 adolescent students 12–16 years old in Israel. Short form (50 items) FES. Sense of Coherence Scale, Social Skills Checklist, Junior Eysenck Personality Questionnaire	The FES relationship and growth clusters as well as gender interactions with both were predictors of Sense of Coherence in multiple regression analysis. Boys with high personal growth scores but girls with low personal growth scores had higher Sense of Coherence scale scores.
McKelvey et al., 1989	Family functioning, diabetes knowledge, family support of self-care activities, metabolic control	89 Teens with diabetes and their families FES, Diabetes-Specific Family Behavior Scale (DFBS), Hemoglobin AbAIC.	Two FES scales (Cohesion and Active - recreational orientation) are positively related and one (Conflict) negatively related to AIC. Adolescents have better control when parents make them feel good about taking care of the diabetes, talk with them about the diabetes, and listen to their problems. Adolescents have worse control if parents let them "get away with more" because of diabetes or argue with them about whether they adhere to the diabetes diet.

Steiner & Levine, 1988	Psychiatric diagnosis, stress; family functioning	10 teen subjects; five DMS-III diagnoses; five without admission to hospital. Plasma Cortisol Assessment FES	Groups differed on physiological stress measure (cortisol) at discharge from hospital. Groups differed by Conflict, Control, and Incongruency on FES. Teens with psychiatric diagnoses had families with increased Conflict, Control, and larger differences in perception of family by teen/parent.
Stuifbergen, 1990	Families with child in which one parent has a chronic illness. Physical and psychosocial symptoms of illness, family functioning.	Purposive sample of 67 parents (31 men, 36 women). Family information sheet, Sickness Impact Profile (SIP), FES	Cluster analysis yielded four FES clusters (Cohesive; Moral-Religious; Structured conflict; Unstructured conflict). The largest number of families fell in Cohesive cluster. Parents in Cohesive cluster had less disruption in sleep/rest, emotional behavior, social interaction, alertness behavior, work, and recreation. Parents in Structured Conflict cluster had greater disruption in rest and sleep, emotional behavior, body control and movement, social interaction, emulation, and alertness behavior. Although few in number, parents experiencing high Conflict and low Cohesion are stressed and may need specific interventions. The proposal that chronic illness has consistent negative impact on families not supported by this study.
Turner, Sloper, Knussen, & Cunningham, 1991	Self-sufficiency in children with Down's syndrome, behavior problems, mental age, excitability, coping, social activity, family functioning.	117 mothers and 87 fathers of children 6-14 years in England. Self-sufficiency Index, Ways of coping Questionnaire, Marlowe-Crowne Social Desirability Scale, ADIECAS scale, teacher and parent's rating inventories, FES.	While 6 subscales of FES were correlated to Self-sufficiency Index, none entered into the multiple regression analysis.
Wallander, Varni, Babani, Banis, & Wilcon, 1989	Psychological adjustment, family functioning, family resources	153 children ages 4-16 and their mothers. Child Behavior Checklist, FES, Family Utilitarian resources.	Cohesion, expressiveness, conflict, organization, and control were FES scales related to Adjustment scales. The largest relationship (multiple regression) was between family cohesion and child social competence after maternal education and family income were entered.

FAMILY APGAR

History

The Family APGAR was created by G. Smilkstein in 1978 as an efficient screening instrument for family functioning in the care of patients and their families. The creator of the instrument assumed that the overall dimension of family functioning could be assessed by five single questions measuring satisfaction with five domains of family functioning. The work on this instrument has taken place within the health professions of medicine and nursing. The Family APGAR was the first instrument developed in this series (Smilkstein, 1978); the Friend APGAR and the Work APGAR (Smilkstein, Ashworth, & Montano, 1982) followed; and the most recent instrument Family APGAR for use by 8-year-olds was an adaption of the original Family APGAR (Austin & Huberty, 1989). The acronym APGAR is universally known in health care settings as a 5-item screening instrument for the status of newborn infants. A Family APGAR, then, is instantly recognizable as a 5-concept screening instrument for the family.

Overview of the Model

This instrument is based on a systems model incorporating stress and change/adaptation in one or more members. Family is defined as a psychosocial group consisting of the patient and one or more person, children or adults, in which there is a commitment for members to nurture each other. Family function refers to the way in which the family is viewed by an individual as a nurturing and supportive unit. The tool allows identification of the individual's perception of the value of the family as a psychosocial resource (high score) or poor social support or possible stressor (Smilkstein, 1992). The model is operationalized by five dimensions: adaptation, partnership, growth, affection, and resolution because they were thought to represent the common themes in the social science literature. Smilkstein (1992) defines the dimensions in the following manner:

Adaptation. The member's satisfaction with the assistance received when family resources are needed.
Partnership. The member's satisfaction with mutuality in family communications and problem-solving.
Growth. The member's satisfaction with freedom available within the family to

change roles and attain emotional growth or maturation.

Affection. The member's satisfaction with the intimacy and emotional interaction within the family.

Resolve. The member's satisfaction with the time* commitment that has been made by the family members. (*Besides sharing time, family members usually have a commitment to share space and money. Because of its primacy, time was the only item included in the revised family APGAR.)

FAMILY APGAR INSTRUMENT DESCRIPTION

The five Likert-type items in part I of the questionnaire are generally administered as a one-page instrument in either the 3- or 5-choice format. The reading level is approximately 10 years of age. It takes less than 5 minutes to complete the instrument.

Scoring. In the 3-choice format, 2 = Almost always; 1 = some of the time; and 0 = never. Scores are totaled. A score of 7-10 suggests good family function. A score of 5-6 suggests a moderately dysfunctional family, and a score of 0 to 4 suggests a highly dysfunctional family. Discrepant scoring (difference between family members) may be used to explore congruency of family members' perceptions. Coding for the 5-point scale recommended for research purposes is: 0 = never, 1 = hardly, 2 = some of the time, 3 = almost always, and 4 = always.

The five items include:

I am satisfied that I can turn to my family for help when something is troubling me.

I am satisfied with the way my family talks over things with me and shares problems with me.

I am satisfied that my family accepts and supports my wishes to take on new activities or directions.

I am satisfied with the way my family expresses affection and responds to my emotion, such as anger, sorrow, or love.

I am satisfied with the way my family and I share time together.

Part II of the Family APGAR Questionnaire addresses the positive and negative aspects of a person's interactions with family members and friends. This section has four questions: (1) Who lives in your home (relationship, age, and sex); (2) Indicate the category (well, fairly, poorly) that describes how you now get along with each member of the family listed; (3) If you don't live with your own family, list the persons to whom you turn for help most frequently (relationship, age, sex); and (4) Indicate the category that best describes how you get along with each person listed in #3 (well, fairly, poorly). This section is also quick to fill out, gives screening information in a timely manner, and has the potential to identify families at risk. No data are reported using Part II in any published report.

PSYCHOMETRIC PROPERTIES

Reliability

Internal Consistency. The instrument operationalizes five different constructs with single item measures and as such may not be expected to have internal consistency, as family members could logically be very satisfied with one aspect and not with another. Cronbach's alphas from the early studies (.80) (Smilkstein et al., 1982) and more recent studies (.90) (Reeb, Graham, Zyzanski, & Kitson, 1987) (.83 to .87) (Gilliss, Neuhaus, & Hauck, 1990), however, have been consistent. These high reliability coefficients support the conclusion that the instrument is really a unidimensional measure of satisfaction with family functioning.

Test–Retest Reliability. A 2-week test–retest reliability (n=100) in a sample of Taiwanese students was .83 using the 5-choice format (Smilkstein et al., 1982).

Inter-Rater Reliability. Not applicable.

Validity

Content Validity. After early studies item 5 was changed. Respondents were asked to respond regarding their satisfaction with the quality rather than the quantity of time spent with family members. The most recent version has minor wording changes in the first two items.

Construct Validity. The initial studies with the instrument were conducted using college students. A second college student sample was used to test the 5-choice format. The increased number of choices increased the standardized mean score, increased the reliability, and increased the item/total correlations. The instrument developer recommended that the 3-choice format be retained for clinical use and the 5-choice format for research. Subsequent studies of 133 new clinic patients yielded mean scores (8.22) very similar to initial validation studies for graduate students but somewhat higher than mean scores for college students (7.35) in study #3 (Smilkstein et al., 1982). In addition, Smilkstein (1993) proposed that the instrument is not a valid measure in highly enmeshed or defensive family members. For example, he predicted that subjects with psychosomatic disease would probably report falsely high scores.

Concurrent Validity. The Family APGAR was correlated with other measures of family functioning in the developmental studies. The APGAR was highly correlated with Pless-Satterwhites Family Functioning Index at $r=.80$ and with therapists' estimates at $r=.64$; correlations between spouses was .67 (Smilkstein et al., 1982). In addition, moderate to large correlations (.48 to .70) were reported with the Feetham Family Functioning Scale, FACES, and Hudson's Family Relations Scale (Smilkstein, 1992).

Predictive Validity. Low APGAR scores predicted postpartum complications in high-risk mothers (Smilkstein, Helsper-Lucas, Ashworth, Montano, & Pagel, 1984).

Discriminant Validity. The original study found that the Family APGAR was able to discriminate between samples of well-adjusted and maladjusted students, with all five items and the total APGAR significantly different.

Additional Data. An altered form of the Family APGAR for use by younger children or children with learning disabilities has been developed by Austin and Huberty (1989), as the original reading/use level was assumed to be at age 10 or above. Items were simplified, but the original structure was followed. For example the first APGAR item was changed from "I am satisfied that I can turn to my family for help when something is troubling me" to "When something is bothering me, I can ask my family for help." The revised instrument was used in two studies. In the first, the original and revised APGAR instruments were both used ($n=50$) approximately 2 weeks apart. Explanations were rarely necessary for the revised questionnaire, the instrument's administration was counterbalanced for order, and an additional instrument was administered in between the two forms to decrease memory of responses to the first APGAR. The 5-point response format was used. Internal consistencies were .71 and .68. Children's scores on the first and second administration were not significantly different. In the second study, 250 children completed the revised APGAR. Cronbach alpha was .70. The authors concluded that the revised APGAR would allow for independent ratings of family functioning by younger children better than the original APGAR.

CROSS-CULTURAL USES, GENDER SENSITIVITY, AND VARIANT FAMILY STRUCTURES

The Family APGAR instrument has been translated and used in several countries. One of the first studies establishing test–retest stability was conducted in Taiwan. Sprusinska and Makowska (1992) studied the effect of social support (Family APGAR) on Polish women's stress and health status and found that occupation was a discriminant factor. Kustner, Vicente, and

Cochoy (1991) studied Granada family functioning in families with and without children with retardation. Chau, Hsiao, Huang, and Liu (1991) and Chung (1990) studied the use of the APGAR in Chinese people. Generally, these authors found the instrument to be a "simple and useful instrument to screen out family dysfunctional patients" (Chau et al., 1991). No norms or psychometric data were available on these studies. Because the instrument measures satisfaction with several general areas, however, it might not have the problems with translations that have plagued the FES. The items do not tap specific behavior, beliefs, or domains, but rather the person's satisfaction. Items that have culture specific descriptors may be at more risk for translation problems than the content-free satisfaction items.

SUMMARY OF STUDIES USING THE FAMILY APGAR

Almost all studies are health related. They address two main agendas: whether family functioning is different in different groups, and whether family functioning as measured by APGAR predicts a variety of health outcomes. In several studies, the FACES scale(s) predicted an outcome, but the Family APGAR did not (see Table 1.4).

CRITIQUE SUMMARY

The Family APGAR is a 5-item screening instrument that measures individual satisfaction on five dimensions. The strength of the instrument is its ease of administration and the focus on perception of satisfaction. Reliability data were positive. The questions raised by the high correlation of APGAR and MMPI-K scale and the questionable sensitivity of the instrument need further investigation. The Family APGAR is predictive of health outcomes for individuals in selected conditions.

SOURCE

Gabriel Smilkstein, MD, Department of Family Practice, School of Medicine, University of California-Davis, TB 152, Davis, California 95616 (or may be obtained from literature cited). Instrument may be reproduced without cost for clinical or research use. A comprehensive manual is available from Dr. Smilkstein (1992).

Table 1.4. Selected Studies Using Family APGAR (FAPGAR)

Author's citation	Variables	Samples/measures	Major findings
Adelman & Shank, 1988	Abdominal pain, family functioning	92 patients presenting with abdominal pain followed for 6 weeks. FAPGAR	Neither age, marital status, sex, education, final diagnoses, occupation, nor family functioning predicted resolution of pain.
Cardenas, Vallbona, Baker, & Yusin, 1987	Family functioning, diabetes control	385 patients were randomly selected from population of individuals with adult-onset diabetes. FAPGAR, HgbAlC	Good family function was found in 92% of those in good control, in 66% of those in fair control, and in only 50% of those in poor control.
Clover, Abell, Becker, Crawford, & Ramsey, 1989	Family function; infection	Prospective cohort sample of adults FACES III, FAPGAR	FACES III scales but not FAPGAR predictive of infections. Findings raise the possibility that family dysfunction may lead to altered immune response which may increase chance of infection.
Fanslow & Shultz, 1991	Differences in perception of family functioning between client caregiver and nurse; Age, sex education	Small convenient sample of families receiving home health care. FAPGAR	No difference found between groups and decrease in FAPGAR scores from time 1 to time 2. Analysis is limited by size of sample.
Foulke, Reeb, Graham, & Zyzanski, 1988	Family function: physician visits for respiratory illness	114 urban black mother-infant pairs followed for first 15 months of infant's life. Hudson's Index of family relationships, FAPGAR, FACES III	Lower family function scores related to higher rates of physician visits for respiratory illness and otitis media.
Gilliss, Neuhaus, & Hauck, 1990	Family functioning; nursing intervention (assumed to be additional resource to family)	Randomized clinical trial of 67 patient-spouse pairs with 3 and 6 months mail follow-up. FAPGAR; FIRM; Marital Adjustment Scale	No differences on FAPGAR by group but scores did decrease at 3 months for both patient and spouse. All patient scores increased at 6 months. General screening tool may not be sensitive to behaviors related to intervention.

(Continued)

39

Table 1.4. Selected Studies Using Family APGAR (FAPGAR) *(Continued)*

Author's citation	Variables	Samples/measures	Major findings
Gwythe, Bentz, Drossman, & Berolzheimer, 1993	Family functioning, Chronic illness, Mental health	Three groups: 58 who sought care for irritable bowel syndrome, 67 with IBS who were not in Treatment, and 73 who did not have IBS FAPGAR, MMPI	Family function scores in normal range for all groups. No difference between groups. FAPGAR was related to the MMPI-K, a defensiveness of test-taking scale. Failure of the APGAR to detect family dysfunction found on interview and relationship to MMPI-K led the authors to question the validity of the FAPGAR.
Leavitt, 1990	Coping with major vascular surgery and recovery. Family functioning.	21 patients and their partners interviewed at predischarge; 72 hours; 2, 4, & 12 weeks. FAPGAR, FCOPES, FIRM, Qualitative interview	FAPGAR scores lower for family member from time 1 to 2 (qualitative data indicate that due to fact that partner sacrificed and accommodated the patient's needs).
McCain, 1990	Selected risk factors as predictors of family function.	Longitudinal study 2-4 years after preterm birth, 55 mothers, 27 fathers. Development status, length of neonatal hospitalization, parental age FDM and FAPGAR	Family Functioning measured by FAPGAR identified no differences between parents and there was no relationship with independent variable. Length of hospitalization was related to FDM Role Conflict subscale. In addition, parents differed significantly, with mothers identified as carrying an unfair amount of family role responsibilities.
Mengel, 1987	Knowledge of family functioning; practice patterns	2 groups of patients in family practice setting. Physicians were told FAPGAR scores of one group. FAPGAR, Chart audit for physician's evaluation of family functioning.	24% of patients had FAPGAR scores reflecting family dysfunction. Chart audit revealed knowledge of FAPGAR did not increase frequency with which physicians evaluated family function. Family members with low FAPGAR scores did not have more psychological symptoms in chart than those without low FAPGARs.
Sahaj et al., 1988	Infertility, life changes, social support, family functioning	134 individuals participating in In-Vitro fertilization program.	Families in the program had high levels of family functioning and normal levels of other psychological measures.
Sawin & Marshall, 1993	Congruence in Parents and Teen perceptions of study variables. Family functioning, hope, decision making, developmental outcomes.	40 teens with chronic illness/disability and their parent. FAPGAR FACES III Harter Self Perception Profile Snyders Hope Scale, Adolescent Psychological Functioning Tool	Parent perceptions of family functioning had only low-moderate correlation to adolescent perception. FAPGAR = .22, FACES III Cohesion = .37, and Adaptability = N.S. Adolescent APGAR (.36) & adolescent cohesion (.46) related to overall self-worth.

(Continued)

Author, Year	Purpose	Sample / Instruments	Findings
Sawin & Marshall, 1992	Factors associated with developmental outcomes in adolescents with spinal cord injury.	Convenient sample of 32 adolescents with spinal cord injury. FAPGAR FACES III Harter Self Perception profile (subscale)	FAPGAR not related to developmental outcomes (FACES III scales related to behavioral outcome).
Shapiro, Neinstein, & Rabinovitz, 1987	Family functioning, suicidal thoughts, mental health, physical health, family problems.	85 teens at Teenage Health Center FAPGAR, screening questionnaire	FAPGAR significantly lower in teens with mental and physical problems, family problems, and those living in residential settings. Validity of screening tool supported in teen population.
Smith, Mayer, Parkhurst, Perkins, & Pingleton, 1991	Caregiver's adaptation to care of ventilator-dependent adult at home.	20 families interviewed FAPGAR, FCOPES	No differences patient/caregivers on FAPGAR. Caregivers reported decreased satisfaction over time. Qualitative data suggest caregivers overwhelmed by caregiving responsibility.
Tishelman, Taube, & Sacks, 1991	Symptom distress in cancer patients, sense of coherence, social support.	Cancer patients in Stockholm Semi-structured interview, McCorkle and Young's Symptom Distress Scale, Antonovsky's Sense of Coherence Questionnaire, Russell's Social Provisions Scale, and FAPGAR	Family functioning, when entered with other psychological variables explained significant amount of variance in symptoms.
Woods, Haberman, & Packard, 1993	Family functioning, demands of illness, family adaptation.	125 women in Family Impact Study Demands of Illness—DOILL (and 7 subscales); Individual Adaptation, CES-D Depression scale, FACES III, FAPGAR, DAS (Dyadic Adaptation Scale)	FACES and FAPGAR both are associated with the family functioning subscale of DOILL (r's=−.32 and −.39). FAPGAR had low but significant relationships with personal demands (body image r=−.16 and personal meaning −.29). Women with more demands directly related to illness had more depression. Women who deal with persistent symptoms may be most at risk for negative outcomes.

FEETHAM FAMILY FUNCTIONING SURVEY
(FFFS)

History

This instrument was developed in the late 1970s by Suzanne Feetham and initially reported by Roberts and Feetham (1982). This team identified the multitude of ways that the concept of family functioning was measured. They chose to base the instrument on the ecological framework for studying families. Although existing instruments addressed the relationship between the family and each individual, the relationship between the family and subsystems and the relationship between the family and the broader community had not been measured. These two later relationships were important to understanding families of children with health problems, a major population of interest to the developer. The instrument addressed all three of these relationships: family to the broader community (such as the work environment or schools); the family and subsystems (such as relatives, friends, and neighbors); and the relationship between family and each individual. The instrument was last revised in 1988.

Overview of Model

The family ecological framework identifies the family as the basic unit. According to Feetham, examining the family using this framework involves explaining the parts, the family's relationships, the environment, the whole and the tasks performed by the family resulting from the relationships of the parts. An assumption is that family functioning is impacted by members' perceptions of the degree that an area is addressed, the expectations one has of the area, the importance one assigns to the area, and the overall satisfaction resulting from whether or not achievement meets the expectations.

FFFS Instrument Description

The FFFS is a 25-item instrument. The items are constructed in the Porter Format, which was originally used to measure individuals' perception of their work situation (Porter, 1962). This format allows for measurement of the discrepancy between the achieved and expected levels and the importance of the item to the respondent. At the same time, the format has been proposed to decrease the risk of social set and social desirability. Porter (1962) does caution, however, that persons with less than a high-school education may have difficulty with this format. The items were created to allow the participant to respond in three domains for each item (How much is there now? How much should there be? and How important is this to me?). The response pattern given to the respondents is a 7-point scale anchored by 'little'(1) to 'much' (7). Even though the 21 items include those that address each of the domains of the conceptual framework, the individual, subsystem, and the broader community, separate scores for each area are not obtained. The instrument also has two open-ended questions: "What is most difficult for you now?" and "What is most helpful for you now?" These items have generated a wealth of qualitative data which have been helpful to a wide variety of investigators. Especially helpful has been the identification of two concepts important to instrument development: satisfaction with family financial status and satisfaction with spirituality (S. Feetham, personal communication, June 1993).

Scoring. Four scores are possible from the instrument: Three direct scores [Is there (A), should there be (B), importance of (C)] and one indirect discrepancy score (D). This discrepancy score is calculated for each family functioning item. Each score is converted to an absolute score to allow the scale score to reflect the magnitude of real differences between items. The discrepancy score for each item is calculated by subtracting "how much there is" (the A factor) from "how much there should be" (the B factor). The range of possible discrepancy scores for each item then becomes 0-6 and the possible discrepancy score for the instrument is 0 to 126. The closer the score is to zero, the less difference between 'what is' and 'what should be.' Feetham felt that the lower the discrepancy score, the more likely that the respondent was satisfied with family function. A high discrepancy score would indicate dissonance among or within the three major areas (individual, greater community, or subsystem) of family functioning. No norms are given for the instrument, although means and standard deviations are reported for each item in the original study. The most recent packet of instructions from the developer of the instrument identifies the discrepancy score as the critical measure of overall family functioning.

Sample Items and Format.

Amount of emotional support from spouse

	Little				Much		
a. How much is there now?	1	2	3	4	5	6	7
b. How much should there be?	1	2	3	4	5	6	7
c. How important is this to me?	1	2	3	4	5	6	7

Amount of time your children miss school

a. How much is there now?	1	2	3	4	5	6	7
b. How much should there be?	1	2	3	4	5	6	7
c. How important is this to me?	1	2	3	4	5	6	7

The amount of: discussion with your friends regarding your concerns; discussion with your relatives regarding your concerns; time you spend with your spouse; discussion of your concerns with your spouse; time you spend with neighbors; time you spend in recreational activities; help from your spouse with family tasks; help from relatives with family tasks; problems with your child(ren); time you spend with your child(ren); disagreements with your spouse; time you are ill; time you spend doing housework; time you miss work; time your spouse misses work; emotional support from friends; emotional support from relatives; time your work routine is disrupted; time your spouse's work routine is disrupted; satisfaction with your marriage; and satisfaction with sexual relations with your spouse.

PSYCHOMETRIC PROPERTIES

The instrument was originally tested with longitudinal and cross-sectional studies of families with infants with and without chronic illness. The original studies were 103 mothers of children with spina bifida; 52 parents of normal 6-month-olds; and 58 parents of normal 18-month-olds. Subsequent samples of 592 parents (using the 21-item format) and 128 parents (using the 25-item format) were used to examine the reliability and validity of the instrument (Feetham & Carroll, 1988). Over 50 studies have used this instrument, and extensive reliability and validity data exist. Current work continues to address psychometric analysis (Faux & Ford-Gilboe, 1993; Zoeller, Knafl, Breitmayer, & Gallo, 1993; Loveland-Cherry & Horan, 1993).

Reliability

Internal Consistency. Well established. Data from the initial instrument development indicated Cronbach alphas of .66 for "what is"; .75 for "what should be"; .84 for importance; and .81 for discrepancy score. Subsequent studies reporting reliability data have usually used the discrepancy score, and report reliability estimates ranging from .78-.82 (Mercer, Ferketich, DeJoseph, May, & Sokkid, 1988) to .78-.80 (Youngblut & Shiao, 1993). In addition, the individual scores also have high reliabilities (Loveland-Cherry, Horan, Burman, Youngblut, & Rogers, 1993). The developer of the instrument reports reliability of .85 on the 25-item instrument, better than the values for the individual factors, which led to the conclusion that there was little support for the use of the factors as subscales (Feetham & Carroll, 1988). No reliability data have been reported for the three factors identified by factor analysis (individual, subsystem, and broader social units) in subsequent studies.

Test–Retest Reliability. Reported in original study as .85 ($n=22$) for 2-week interval.

Inter-Rater Reliability. Not applicable.

Validity

Content Validity. The items generated from the literature and clinical experience were reviewed by a two-phase process. First, two panels, one with clinical expertise and one with family theory expertise, reviewed the instrument. Second, a pilot study was conducted with families who also critiqued the instrument for clarity, format, and language. The final instrument reflects feedback from the process.

Construct Validity. Factor Analysis (varimax rotation) using data from the original instrument development study ($n=103$) supported the three conceptual domains (individual, subsystem, and broader social units). Items loading above .43 were included. Eighteen of the 21 items loaded on the three factors, but all items were retained for further testing. Subsequent analysis on samples using both the 21- and 25-item instrument supported three orthogonal factors (Feetham & Carroll, 1988). Only one study (Sawyer, 1992) examined scores on the individual, subsystem, and broader social units subscales identified by factor structure. They reported there was no significant difference between families with children who had cystic fibrosis and those with healthy children. Convergence of qualitative and quantitative data gives support to the construct validity of the FFFS (Faux & Ford-Gilboe, 1993; Zoeller et al., 1993).

Concurrent Validity. Initial studies compared the FFFS to the Family Functioning Index (-.54) (Roberts & Feetham, 1982). Later studies continued to support concurrent validity, indicating that the FFFS discrepancy score had relationships of -.53 and -.56 with the FACES II Adaption and Cohesion scales, -.68 with the Family Functioning Index, -.54 with the Family APGAR and -.51 with the Family Satisfaction Scale (Feetham, 1991b), -.45 with Family hardiness, -.22 with the CHIP I scale (maintaining psychological stability), .27 with the Family Stress Index, and .32 with the loss dimension of social support (Failla & Jones, 1991). In the latter study these low to moderate relationships were interpreted as appropriate, because each of the instruments measured only the individual aspect of family functioning, not the other domains of the FFFS.

Discriminant Validity. None reported.

Predictive Validity. Initial longitudinal studies indicated that there was an increase in discrepancy scores for both parents at each of five time intervals (birth, 3 months, 6 months, 12 months, and 18 months).

CROSS-CULTURAL USES, GENDER SENSITIVITY, AND VARIANT FAMILY STRUCTURES

The instrument has been translated into Japanese, French, Korean, and American Sign Language. No studies have been published using these translated instruments to date.

SUMMARY OF STUDIES USING THE FFFS

Most studies have used the discrepancy score, with only one study reporting subscales identified by factor analysis (Sawyer, 1992). The literature is divided into two types of studies: Those using the FFFS to examine differences between identified groups on family functioning, and those examining predictors of family functioning. Generally, there are no differences between most groups (i.e., families with children who have cystic fibrosis and those who are healthy), with high-risk (versus low-risk) pregnant women being the exception. Predictors of family functioning differed by risk status but included social support, negative life events, depression, and parent-infant attachment. For a summary of studies using the FFS, see Table 1.5.

CRITIQUE SUMMARY

The FFFS' strengths are numerous. The instrument has been constructed carefully and tested in over 50 studies. Psychometric work and work with culturally diverse populations continue. Further, the instrument is fairly easy to administer and captures several constructs of family functioning. Psychometric data are encouraging. It is unique in its attempt to measure subsystem and larger units' relationship to the family. The length of the instrument makes it potentially useful in the clinical setting. The limitations of the instrument are the high readability level and the potential for negative reaction from single-parent families. The first limitation can be addressed by reading the items to the subjects. There are no significant differences in the distribution of responses attributed to method of administration (Roberts & Feetham, 1982). Thus, if resources are available and the reading level is a problem, use of the interview method is a viable option.

Feetham proposes that the instrument can measure family functioning in single-parent families. Instrument instructions indicate "The term spouse refers to your husband or wife or the person who assumes the functions of a spouse. If you do not have a person in the spouse role answer the questions based on how much you want the functions met." For example, if the subject does not expect to have a person in the spouse role, then the discrepancy score (what is—how much should be there) could be very low and still accurately reflects satisfaction with family functioning for that subject. Further, if a parent wanted spousal support and did not have it, the lack of satisfaction would be reflected in the high discrepancy score. It is possible that single parents not in a current relationship might react negatively to a family functioning instrument where 9 of the 25 items ask about spouse/marriage. The tool has been used, however, with numbers of single-parent families and subjects did not report difficulty with the content (S. Feetham, personal communication, June 1993).

Future work on this instrument needs to explore the reliability and validity of the individual, subsystem, and wider social unit subscales and their utility. In addition, analysis of the importance scale is missing from the reported literature. If not useful, consideration should be given to removing this scale from the instrument if administration time is an issue.

SOURCE

Feetham Family Functioning Survey (FFFS) Manual, Nursing Research and Development, Division of Nursing and Patient Services, Children's National Medical Center, 111 Michigan Ave. NW, Washington, DC 20010-2970, (301) 402-1446. An information packet is available for $7.00, and individual instruments cost $1.00 each plus postage (copyright). Requests for materials should be directed to the Children's National Medical Center address; Dr. Feetham can be contacted at (301) 402-1466.

Table 1.5. Selected Studies Using the Feetham Family Functioning Scale (FFFS)

Author's citation	Variables	Samples/measures	Major findings
Failla & Jones, 1991	Family stress, family hardiness, coping, support. Satisfaction with family functioning.	Convenient sample of 57 mothers of developmentally delayed child. FFFS, Family Hardiness (FH), Coping Health Inventory for Parents (CHIP), Norbeck Social Support.	Discrepancy score (FFFS) of family satisfaction predicted by FH, Support, parental age, and family stressors (R^2=.42)
Faux & Ford-Gilboe, 1993	Family functioning, hardiness, quality of life	15-month study of 101 developmentally disabled adults. FFFS, FAPGAR, FHI, and Quality of Life (QOL) Scales.	Family functioning scales moderately related (r=.42 to .48); only FHI related to QOL (r=.57).
Knecht, 1991	Mothers' mood states, family functioning, support, home apnea monitoring	Studied 124 mothers from 1st week on monitor until 3 months after discharge (Six contact times) FFFS, Profile of Mood States (POMS), Family Inventory of Resources for Management (FIRM), HHPS (professional support)	For total sample no difference on most study variables by type of provider; Mood generally improved over time. Resources and support predicted mood at T1-5. Resources and support predicted discrepancy FFFS when child on monitor but not when child off monitor.
Loveland-Cherry, Horan, Burman, Youngblut, & Rogers, 1993	Family functioning, well-being of mothers and fathers, implications of differing types of analysis (individual, mean or discrepant scores)	Secondary analysis of 125 sets of parents of preterm infants. FACES III, FFFS, ABS (Affects Balance Scale of Parental Well-Being Scale	Effects of Family variables different for two parents with individual scores; Individual and mean scores accounted for more of the variance in parents' ABS than did discrepancy scores (individual scores predict individual well-being). Discrepancy scores better predictors for mothers than fathers.
Mercer, Ferketich, DeJoseph, May, & Sokkid, 1988	Stress impact on family functioning.	153 High-risk women, 75 partners; 218 low-risk women and 147 of their partners. FFFS, Norbeck's Life Experience survey.	High-risk women reported less optimal family functioning than low-risk women. Partners in the high-risk group had similar family functioning. In low-risk population, partners had lower discrepant family functioning than the women. Different patterns of variables predicted family functioning in high- and low-risk women.
Mercer & Ferketich, 1990	Predictors of family functioning 8 months after birth of child (stress, gender, risk status, depression), general health status, sense of mastery, state trait anxiety, CDC Depression scale.	Convenience sample of 353, 83 high-risk women, 45 partners; 139 low-risk women and 82 partners. Recruited during pregnancy. FFFS, Norbeck's Life Experience survey.	High-risk families' function predicted by depression, support, marital status, age, and close friends. Low-risk families had similar patterns, but also included attachment, and negative life events.

Nicholson et al., 1993	Families with adult in ICU. Child visit intervention. Child anxiety, family function, and perceived change.	Twenty families; manifest anxiety scale FFFS	Children in intervention group had reduction in negative behavior and anxiety. No difference between groups in family functioning.
Sawyer, 1992	Family functioning when children have cystic fibrosis (CF).	32 mothers with child with CF and 32 mothers with comparison child. FFFS	No difference in family functioning between families with and without cystic fibrosis.
Sweeney, 1988	Impact of primary caretakers in two groups of infants with apnea (monitored and nonmonitored)	Twenty-one caretaker pairs surveyed at three time periods. FFFS, Mood Survey, and Impact on family-scale.	No difference in family function by groups. Low discrepancy scores indicate fairly high satisfaction with family functioning in this high-risk group.
Youngblut, Loveland-Cherry, & Horan, 1991	Mother's employment status, satisfaction with employment or family functioning.	110 families from Level 2 ICUs. FFFS, FACES, Bailey, home/employment orientation	No significant differences across employment groups on family functioning and child development. Infant development positively correlated with employment and choice for employed mothers.
Youngblut, Loveland-Cherry, & Horan, 1993	Family functioning, attitudes about maternal employment, employment status, and child development outcomes.	Longitudinal study of preterm infants. This sample (67) had mothers with same employment status at 3 and 9 months. Home/employment Orientation Scale (HEO), FACES III, FFFS, Bayley Scales	None of 3 or 6 month family measures associated with employment-related variables. Consistency between employment attitudes at 3 and 6 months predicted employment variables. FFFS Cohesion/Adaptability in nonemployed group decreased from T1-T3. Maternal employment attitude/behavior consistency significant predictor of psychomotor development. Choice in employment at 3 months related to development at 9 and 12 months for nonemployed mothers.
Youngblut & Shiao, 1993	Child behaviors, family function, parental stressor.	Nine mothers and fathers of children after child discharged from PICU. FFFS and FACES III	PICU admission is stressful for parents regardless of illness severity. Mothers' perceptions of family may be negatively affected.

2
Moderately Established Self-Report Instruments

THE FAMILY ASSESSMENT MEASURE (FAM III)

History

The Process Model of Family Functioning and the McMaster Model included in this review initially emanated from the Family Categories Schema (Epstein, Rakoff, & Sigal, 1968) and integrate different approaches to family therapy and research. Although there is considerable conceptual similarity between the McMaster and Process Models related to the dimensions that are considered essential to understanding a family as a system, the Process Model of Family Functioning places greater emphasis on family dynamics, specifically the interaction of the individual family and the family in its social environment, while identifying family strengths and weaknesses across three levels (Skinner, Steinhauer, & Santa-Barbara, 1983). Refinement of the theoretical process model (Steinhauer, 1984, 1987) operationalized by the Family Assessment Measure III continues at the Departments of Behavioral Science and Psychiatry at the University of Toronto, Canada.

Overview of the Model

Family functioning is characterized as a set of systems processes versus family structures aimed at the overall goal of accomplishing certain tasks categorized as basic, developmental, or crisis related. A major assumption is that a family's existence rests on the individual members' sharing common goals that provide for the biological, psychological, social development, and maintenance of family members. Although the necessary tasks to reach these goals vary across the family life cycle, there are certain skills and similar processes regardless of a particular family life stage (Steinhauer, Santa-Barbara, & Skinner, 1984).

In order to complete the necessary tasks to reach the common goals, success in six other process dimensions (constructs) is necessary. These include: Role Performance, Communication, Affective Expression, Affective Involvement, Control, and Values and Norms. Assessment of each of these dimensions is done at both the total family system and individual intrapsychic levels

(Steinhauer & Tisdall, 1984). Role performance assesses the allocation, agreement among members, and actual enactment of family activities. Communication assesses the clarity of the message sent and openness to receiving messages. Affective Expression measures the range, quality, and appropriateness of expressed feelings. Affective Involvement assesses the degree to which individuals are interested in each other. Control relates to processes of influence and control of each others' behaviors. Finally, Values and Norms reflects the cultural and familial determinants of how tasks are defined and enacted.

Instrument Description

The Family Assessment Measure III operationalizes the Process Model of Family Functioning, and was developed according to a construct validation paradigm (Skinner, 1987). The present version comprises 134 items that assess the family at three different levels. The General Scale consists of 50 items designed to assess the health/pathology of the family as a whole. Within this scale are two measures of response style biases: Social Desirability and Defensiveness (Skinner, 1987). The Dyadic Relationship Scale consists of 42 items designed to assess the relationships among each dyad (parent–child, brother–sister, etc.) in the family across the seven dimensions denoted as subscales. The Self-Rating Scale consists of 42 items that measure an individual family member's perception of his/her functioning within the family. The FAM III is used as a clinical diagnostic instrument, a measure of therapy outcome, and as a research instrument to measure basic family processes. The FAM is designed to be used with children as young as 10–12 years of age. It takes about 30-45 minutes to complete.

Scoring. A 4-point Likert-style scale records the respondent's choices with an equal number of healthy and pathological keyed responses for each of the seven subscales for the three levels. Responses to each of the three scales provide an overall scale index, as well as a measure for each of the seven dimensions (subscales) that comprise the constructs of the process model. Separate measures for Social Desirability and Defensiveness can be obtained from the General Scale. The three scales can be used independently if a more comprehensive assessment of the family at all three levels is not needed. The FAM III takes between 30 and 45 minutes to complete and is designed for use by respondents at least 10 years of age.

A hand-scorable version is available, and responses can be graphed on a profile sheet. Computerized scoring is also available (IBM-PC microcomputer compatible). An Administration and Interpretation Guide is available, which includes normative data separately for adults ($n=247$) and adolescents ($n=65$) from nonclinical families. Additional normative data for clinical samples representing over 2,000 individuals also are available (see "Source" at the end). Clinical families include members with various physical and psychiatric difficulties.

Sample Items. (level represented)

"We spend too much time arguing what our problems are." (General Scale)
"This person worries too much about me." (Dyadic Scale)
"I often don't understand what other family members are saying." (Self-Rating Scale)

PSYCHOMETRIC PROPERTIES

The original version of the FAM was based on data from 433 individuals representing 182 clinical and nonclinical families.

Reliability

Internal Consistency. Substantial internal consistency (coefficient alpha) is reported. Based on data from 475 families (933 adults and 502 children), scale reliabilities were .93 (General Scale); .95 (Dyadic Relationships Scale); and .89 (Self-Rating Scale). Scale reliabilities varied by the number of items, with the General Scale subscales having fewer items reporting a median reliability of .73, for the Dyadic Relationships subscales, .72, and for the Self-Rating subscales, .53. The intercorrelations ranges by subscale were: .39-.70 for the General Scale; .63-.82 for the Dyadic Relationships Scale; and .25-.63 for the Self-Rating Scale (Jacob & Tennenbaum, 1988; Skinner, 1987).

Test–Retest. No reported evidence.

Inter–Rater Reliability. Not applicable.

Validity

Content Validity. The FAM was developed using the construct validation paradigm (Skinner, 1987). Starting with an explicit definition of each construct in the Process Model, a pool of over 800 items was generated and rated for clarity, content saturation, and clinical relevance. For each of the seven subscales representing each construct, the best 30 items were selected to constitute the preliminary version of the FAM. Each subscale was balanced for healthy/pathological keyed responses to a 5-point scale. Three scales (Social Desirability, Defensiveness, and Family Conventionalization) were added to test for response style biases.

Construct Validity. The discriminatory power of each item, scale reliability, intercorrelation among scales, and the influence of the response-style bias were tested through the analysis of FAM test data obtained from 433 persons representing 182 clinical and nonclinical families (Skinner, Santa-Barbara, & Steinhauer, 1981). Median internal consistency reliabilities were .93 for the

30-item subscales and .87 for the best 10 items of each subscale. Intercorrelations for the subscales ranged from .55 to .79. These data were used to develop a briefer 15-item instrument, FAM-II, which was used in several studies. Based on feedback obtained from researchers using the FAM-II and further statistical analyses indicating that the family needed to be assessed from three different levels, FAM-III was devised (Halvorsen, 1991; Skinner, 1987).

Concurrent Validity. In studies that compared data reported by wives to those of their spouses for clinical and nonclinical samples, the results paralleled those reported in similar studies using FACES II (Olson & Portner, 1983). Other concurrent validity evidence was not found in materials used for this review.

Discriminant Validity. The FAM III was found to adequately discriminate between clinical and nonclinical families (n=475). Clinical families included those involved in individual or family treatment for psychiatric, emotional, alcohol, drug, school-related, or major legal problems, which together represented 28% of the total families. "A multiple discriminant analysis was conducted to identify linear combinations of subscales from the General Scale that significantly differentiated among (a) problem versus non-problem families and (b) family position (father, mother, and child)" (Skinner, 1987, p. 443). When compared to responses from adults, children were more likely to report problems in the areas of Control, Values and Norms, and Affective Expression. Also, when problem families were compared to nonproblem families there was a greater tendency for the problem families to report more dysfunction in the areas of Role Performance and Involvement. Overall, when compared to fathers or children in clinical and nonclinical families, mothers rated their families in the hypothesized direction to a greater degree (Skinner et al., 1983).

Predictive Validity. No additional evidence reported.

Other: Social Desirability and Defensiveness. Using data from 475 families consisting of 933 adults and 502 children, moderate relationships using median correlations between social desirability and the scales were: -.53 for the General Scale; -.35 for the Dyadic Relationships Scale; and -.35 for the Self-Rating Scale. Median correlations with Defensiveness were slightly lower: -.48 for General Rating Scale; -.28 for the Dyadic Relationships Scale; and -.28 for the Self-Rating Scale (Skinner et al., 1983).

CROSS-CULTURAL USES, GENDER SENSITIVITY, AND VARIANT FAMILY STRUCTURES

A fair amount of evidence indicates that there are gender differences within families when responses from fathers and mothers are compared. In a 1983 study using FAM II (Garfinkel et al., 1983), mothers and daughters reported significantly increased dysfunction in Task Accomplishment, Role Performance, Communication, and Affective Expression in the anorexia group compared to a control group. In contrast, fathers tended to report better or higher functioning than did mothers or daughters in both groups.

The FAM III is only available in English. It has been used in research in populations with medical, substance abuse, psychiatric, child welfare (adoption and foster care), and school difficulties.

SUMMARY OF STUDIES USING THE FAM III

The Family Assessment Measure has been used in research related to school-aged children; mental health difficulties; physical illness and disability; alcohol dependency; and child welfare areas. The focus of much of the research is on understanding the relationship of the individual illness or concern to the functioning of the person's family. A summary of studies using the FAM III is found in Table 2.1.

CRITIQUE SUMMARY

The FAM III provides a uniquely comprehensive understanding of family dynamics at the whole family, dyadic, and individual levels. Consequently, if the entire instrument consisting of 132 items is used, it is lengthy, particularly if each family member rates his/her relationship with all other family members by repeating the Dyadic Scale for each dyad. Whereas response style biases are typically reported as part of the normative data for an instrument and assumed to generalize to other families assessed with the same instrument, for the FAM III both social desirability and defensiveness can be assessed each time the instrument is used, since marker variables are a part of the General Scale. As with other self-report instruments, the obtained data represent individual family members' perceptions versus possibly more objective data that a clinical rater may obtain. On the other hand, measuring perceptual similarities or differences may be the desired outcome of the researcher or clinician on which to base intervention or to measure treatment outcome. Since there was a heavy reliance on nonclinical families for normative data, information for clinical families may be limited.

SOURCE

Information about obtaining copies of FAM-III and an administration and interpretation manual is available by contacting Multi-Health Systems, Inc.,

65 Overlea Blvd., Suite 210, Toronto, Ontario, Canada, M4H1P1, or calling 1-800-456-3003 (USA) or 1-800-268-6011 (Canada) or FAX (416) 424-1736. Information regarding current research and clinical applications of FAM-III can be obtained by contacting the test author, Harvey Skinner, Ph.D., Professor and Chairman, Department of Behavioral Science, McMurrich Building, Toronto, Ontario, M5S 1A8. Telephone: (416) 978-8989 for voice mail; (416) 978-2087 for FAX. The FAM-III Specimen Set (includes 1 of each test booklet, 5 General Scale answer sheets, 10 Dyadic Relationship Scale answer sheets, 5 Self-Rating Scale answer sheets, 2 General Scale Profile sheets, 5 Dyadic Relationship/Self-Rating Scale Profile sheets, 1 Administration and Interpretation Guide) is $20.00. The FAM-III Starter Kit (includes 10 of each test booklet, 50 General Scale answer sheets, 75 Dyadic Relationship Scale answer sheets, 50 Self-Rating Scale answer sheets, 25 General Scale Profile sheets, 50 Dyadic Relationship/Self-Rating Scale Profile sheets, 1 Administration and Interpretation Guide) is $95.00. Packages of 10 reusable booklets are $7.00 for each of the scales; 25 answer sheets are $10.00 for each of the scales. The Administration and Interpretation Guide is $10.00.

THE FAMILY DYNAMICS MEASURE

History

The Family Dynamics Measure (FDM) was created by a family interest group of nurse researchers in the early 1980s. This team, which began as a work group in the Midwest Nursing Research Society, embarked on developing this instrument after reviewing the literature. The review yielded no instrument measuring the family dynamics domains most meaningful to the nursing profession (Lasky et al., 1985). Specifically, these researchers felt that holistic family assessment was not addressed. The group was interested in developing an instrument that was fairly comprehensive, that could encompass varying family structures, and that was easy to read. After reviewing several conceptual approaches to family dynamics, the Barnhill framework of healthy family systems was chosen and the instrument development begun. Instrument refinement has continued over the last 10 years (Fitzgerald, Speer, & Trevor, 1988; P. Wilson, personal communication, 1992). The instrument has been used primarily by a Research Team at the University of Florida and their colleagues in the US-Nordic Family Dynamics Nursing Research Project. Current work is directed toward international use of the instrument.

Overview of the Model

Family functioning as conceptualized by Barnhill (1979) is reflected by four themes with eight specific dimensions of healthy functioning. The themes of

Table 2.1. Selected Studies Using Family Assessment Measure (FAM III)

Author's citation	Variables	Samples/measures	Major findings
Bernstein, Svingen, & Garfinkel, 1990	School phobia	76 families of phobic children. FAM III (total)	Mother and father rated significant dysfunction in Roles, Values & Norms; no difference between intact & single parent ratings; less rated dysfunction by mother & children if diagnosis=anxiety disability vs. school phobia.
Bernstein & Garfinkel, 1988	School phobia, pedigrees, & family functioning.	Family pedigree of 6 children with phobia compared to 5 matching families with psychiatric diagnosis. Structured interview & FAM III (total)	More depression & anxiety disability in 1st-degree relatives of phobic children; more Role, Communication, Affective Expression, & continued family dysfunction with phobics.
Cohen & Westhues, 1990	Adoption outcome, foster/ adoption training, & family functioning.	18-month study of 61 children. FAM III, Community Resources Inventory, & child measures.	Training based on McMaster Model; significantly less family functioning decline in Affective Expression, Involvement, & Roles with training; husbands with lower Communication Value & Norms; wives with less Social Desirability & more positive Role Performance; pre-placement family functioning regained by 18 months.
Cowen et al., 1985	Cystic fibrosis, psychosocial adjustment, & family functioning.	Parents of 41 preschoolers with cystic fibrosis, and 31 healthy children. FAM III, PBQ (Preschool Behavioral Questionnaire) & PINV (Problem Inventory).	More reported problems with healthy children.
Garfinkel et al., 1983	Anorexia nervosa, family characteristics, & functioning.	Anorexia nervosa, family characteristics, & functioning.	FAM III differentiated anorexics from normals.
Simmons et al., 1987	Cystic fibrosis, latency age children.	108 age 6-11 children and their parents. Piers-Harris Self Concept Scale; Children's Health Locus of Control; Child Behavior Checklist. FAM III	23% of children with significant behavior problems; latency vs. preschool and males vs. females had more problems; good social competence and self-concept noted as compensatory mechanisms but with patterns that varied by gender.
Trute, 1990	Parent, child, marital, & family characteristics.	88 families with developmental disabilities child; FAM III, DAS, CCTI, Disability Index	Marital adjustment & education of father related to family functioning; family functioning not related to child attributes.
Van Ripper, Ryff, & Pridham, 1992	Impact of Down's syndrome child on individual, marital, and family functioning.	34 families with Down's syndrome child compared to 41 families with normal child; FAM III (Dyadic Relationship Scale and General Scale); Center for Epidemiological Studies Depression Scale.	No significant difference between groups on individual, marital, or family measures.

a healthy family include: Identity Process; Change; Information Processing; and Role Structure. Each theme is further defined by two bipolar dimensions. Identity includes the dimensions of Individuation-Enmeshment and Mutuality-Isolation. Change consists of Flexibility-Rigidity and Stability-Disorganization. In contrast, Information Processing consists of Clear perceptions-Unclear perceptions and Clear communication-Unclear communication. Finally, the last theme, Role Structure, is made up of Role reciprocity-Role conflict and Clear generational boundaries-Diffuse generational boundaries. Sample definitions are given for four of the six dimensions (Brackbill, White, Wilson, & Kitch, 1990):

> INDIVIDUATION: Independence of thought, feelings, and judgment of individual family members; a firm sense of autonomy, personal responsibility, identity, and boundaries of self. ENMESHMENT: Poorly delineated boundaries of self, and identity, dependent on others, symbiosis and shared ego fusion.
>
> MUTUALITY: Sense of emotional closeness, joining, or intimacy which is only possible between individuals with clearly defined entities. ISOLATION: Alienation or disengagement from others. Isolation can occur either with enmeshment or with isolated withdrawal from family relationship.
>
> STABILITY: Consistency, responsibility, and security in family interactions. DISORGANIZATION: Lack of stability or consistency in family relations; lack of predictability and clear responsibility.
>
> ROLE RECIPROCITY: Mutually agreed upon behavior patterns or sequences in which an individual complements the role of a partner. ROLE CONFLICT: Lack of clearly agreed upon behavioral complementarity between family members; results in unclear and confusing role behavior or persistent conflict among the poorly defined role-orientated behaviors.

Barnhill indicated that in healthy families the dimensions are interactive such as in a system where change in one effects change in the other. Family dynamics were defined as "the unique ways family members relate within the family" (Tomlinson, White, & Wilson, 1990, p. 684). Barnhill compares the concept of mutuality with cohesion in the family unit. Six of the dimensions were chosen by the instrument developers for the FDM instrument. The dimensions 'perceptions' and 'generational boundaries' were not operationalized.

FDM Instrument Description

The Family Dynamics Measure is a 62-item questionnaire with a 6-point Likert-type format (from strongly agree to strongly disagree). The items are randomly ordered and are both positively and negatively stated items. There are not an equal number of items per dimension. The instrument was revised after validity and reliability studies (Fitzgerald et al., 1988) to increase the clarity of items. The instrument can be administered to those with a third-grade reading level. The instrument has been used both in a pencil and paper format and in an interview format. Administration time is 20 minutes or less. The instrument is based on the assumption that two or more adults are in the family.

Scoring. A 6-point Likert-type scale is used to record the respondent's choice. The most positive responses are given a value of 1 and the least, a value of 6. Scale scores are created by summing the scale items after reversing negative items.

Sample Items. All items start with the stem, "In my family":

When I feel blue, someone comforts me (mutuality).
I feel left out (isolation).
Each of us can do the same job in different ways (flexibility).
Once a decision is made, it's hard to change (rigidity).
I know what to expect from other members (stability).
I cannot count on how family money will be spent (disorganization).

PSYCHOMETRIC PROPERTIES

Several studies that address reliability and validity are reported on this instrument. Work is also in process to further develop the psychometric evidence for this instrument.

Reliability

Internal Consistency. Initial reliabilities for the scales were: Individuation, .48; Flexibility, .64; Role, .76; Communication, .88; Stability, .85; and Mutuality, .88. Reliabilities varied considerably, however, across the three initial samples. Internal consistency of the FDM has been reported in subsequently published studies (for the six dimensions of the FDM) as "median" Cronbach's alpha of .79 in Florida (Tomlinson et al., 1990), .72 in Iceland (Tómasdóttir, Wilson, White, & Ágústsdóttir, 1991), and .84 in Denmark (Wilson, Hall, & White, 1994). Communication with the Florida Research Team currently using the instrument (White & Elander, 1992) provided scale specific data. All scales except Flexibility-Rigidity and Individuation-Enmeshment had Cronbach alphas above .74. The Individuation-Enmeshment and the Flexibility-Rigidity scales consistently have low reliabilities despite item revisions described in Lasky et al. (1985). Readers who are interested in these dimensions of the instrument need to proceed with caution. Further validity studies are currently being planned to identify items to strengthen those two scales (M. White, personal communication, September 1993).

Test–Retest Reliability. No data are available. The University of Florida Research team currently is conducting an additional psychometric study.

Inter-Rater Reliability. Not applicable.

Validity

Content Validity. The original version of the FDM was created in a multistage process. Item generation was bounded by two criteria, timelessness and universality. First, the item needed to refer to all stages of family life and levels of function, and second, it had to meet the criteria of applicability across cultures, types of families, and levels of health. Items were generated by group consensus. The development of the 112 items was guided by the criteria and conceptual framework. Content validity was reviewed by a panel of experts in family therapy and nursing. Experts were asked to sort items by conceptual category as needed. Items that did not reach 80% agreement were eliminated. Additional items were generated and reviewed for exclusivity and internal consistency with categories. The next step in establishing content validity included a pilot using 'normal families.' Respondents completed the questionnaire and were asked to identify items that gave them difficulty or were unclear. Items were changed or omitted if 90% of the subjects selected an extreme response. The final content validity check was done by 13 family therapists. They were asked to (1) indicate if the item responded to one of Barnhill's dimensions; (2) give specific suggestions regarding the item; (3) identify unclear or inappropriate items; (4) determine if the item was relevant for practice; (5) identify potential uses for the instrument. Five items were revised, two items were felt by 60% of the therapists to be unclear, and three other items were viewed as having marginal clarity. Seventy percent was the cutoff point for agreement between therapists and resulted in modification of eight items.

Construct Validity. Three samples were used to explore construct validity, 116 college faculty and students and their respective families; 364 parent subjects who had experienced the birth of a high-risk newborn; and 144 couples in which one member had a chronic illness. Item-scale correlations, item means, standard deviations, alpha reliability coefficient (for scale), response scale midpoint, and number of items in the scale were reviewed. Factor analysis of the high-risk and normal families ($n=608$) confirmed six factors. The original high-risk family study demonstrated no significant difference in scale means between mothers and fathers. Several of the scales were moderately (i.e., $r=.35$, .45, .55) to highly (i.e., $r=.67$, .81) correlated. This raises the question whether the highly correlated subscales (Mutuality and Communication; Stability and Communication) are really distinct subscales. An alternative proposal is that Communication is the 'index' subscale, as it correlated at least .38 with all other scales. These correlations may present problems in multivariate analysis. Future users of the instrument may want to analyze the factor structure of the scale scores to see if there are any higher-level dimensions represented.

Discriminant Validity. In the original set of studies, the normal families differed consistently from the high-risk newborn or chronic illness samples (Lasky et al., 1985).

CROSS-CULTURAL USES, GENDER SENSITIVITY, AND VARIANT FAMILY STRUCTURES

This instrument has one of the most extensive cross-cultural uses. It has been translated for use in Iceland, Denmark, Sweden, Finland, Estonia, and Norway. The back translation method has been used for this process. In this method one author translates the instrument, for example to Danish. A content expert group (Danish nursing faculty in Hall, Wolff, White, & Wilson, 1993) reviews the instrument for accuracy of translation. Then, a second translator unfamiliar with the original English version of the instrument translates the instrument back to English. Differences in meaning are then resolved between the translators and authors fluent in the non-English language. Reliabilities need to be closely examined in translated instruments. The intent of items needs to be examined carefully. The concept, not the word, is the critical factor (White & Elander, 1992). Hall et al. (1993) propose that the internal reliability coefficients of the six dimensions support the validity of the FDM in the Nordic languages used. A validation study is underway in Iceland to address the instrument's cross-cultural validity. The instrument has been created to accommodate a variety of family structures.

SUMMARY OF STUDIES USING THE FDM

These studies indicate that there are gender differences within families when responses from fathers and mothers are compared. The most recent study (Denmark) had the largest sample of mother/father pairs (99 mothers and 84 fathers). In the studies conducted to date, family structure (married, cohabiting, engaged, and living with adult other than partner) was used in analysis. Due to small numbers in some cells, data were often collapsed to married/nonmarried. However, the instrument is appropriate for families with a variety of structures. The phenomenon most frequently explored with this instrument is family functioning in families with newborns. This body of research, using prenatal measures of family functioning and subsequent child temperament, supports the impact of family functioning (specifically stability versus disorganization) on infant temperament. For a summary of studies using the FDM see Table 2.2.

CRITIQUE SUMMARY

The FDM provides an instrument that has been successfully used to measure family functioning in cross-cultural samples. The tool is appropriate for families with a variety of structures. It has a reading level (third grade) appropriate for wide use. The lack of extensive data on validity and reliability and the questionable reliability of select scales are a potential weakness that hopefully will be addressed in the near future.

SOURCE

Dr. Marjorie White, University of Florida, College of Nursing, Box 100187 HSC, Gainesville, FL 32610.

FAMILY HARDINESS INDEX (FHI)

History

This 20-item instrument was developed to measure the characteristic of hardiness conceptualized as a mediating factor or buffer to family stress (McCubbin, McCubbin, & Thompson, 1987a). Hardiness thus would mitigate the effects of stress of family adjustment and adaptation. The family hardiness concept was based on the concept of individual hardiness. The FHI was initially used in a study of 304 nonclinical families as a part of the ongoing research of the Family Stress Coping and Health Project at the University of Wisconsin-Madison. The creators of the instrument come from the disciplines of Nursing and Family Studies and currently continue the development of both the model and instruments at the Family Stress Coping and Health Project at the University of Wisconsin-Madison. The FHI was first introduced in the text *Family Assessment Inventories for Research and Practice* (1987) and has been used in a limited number of published reports and numerous dissertations. The majority of the studies have looked at families undergoing a major medical or psychosocial stressor.

OVERVIEW OF THE MODEL

This instrument is one of several created to measure concepts in a model of family transitions, crisis, and adaption articulated by McCubbin and McCubbin (1987). Originally called The T-Double ABCX Model of Family Adjustment and Adaptation (McCubbin & McCubbin, 1987), and more recently renamed The Resiliency Model of Family Stress, Adjustment and Adaptation (McCubbin & McCubbin, 1993), this model identifies stressors, family types, resources, and outcomes for both acute (Adjustment) and long-term stressors (Adaptation). In this model family typology is analogous to family functioning: a set of basic attributes about the family system that characterizes and explains how a family system typically appraises, operates, and/or behaves. The authors propose that family type is the predictable and discernible pattern of family

Table 2.2. Selected Studies Using the Family Dynamics Measure (FDM)

Author's citation	Variables	Samples/measures	Major findings
Brackbill, White, Wilson, & Kitch, 1990	Infant Temperament. Family dynamics, social status, age, education.	87 women having first baby and 73 women having second child. FDM, Revised Infant Temperament Questionnaire (RITQ), Björnsson-Edelstein Scale of Occupational Class.	Stability-Disorganization family dynamics scale accurately classified infants by temperament. Although social status was associated with temperament, more stable, organized families had infants with easier disposition regardless of SES.
Hall, Wolff, White, & Wilson, 1993	Family structure, family dynamics, social status, age.	158 mothers and 126 fathers in third trimester of low-risk pregnancy in Denmark. FDM; Danish Social Classification, Danish National Institute for Social Research	Married mothers reported more Mutuality, Stability, and clearer communication; fathers more Mutuality. Mothers with higher social status had more Individuation. Mothers reported families as more individuated and flexible, while fathers indicated more role reciprocity.
Tómasdóttir, Wilson, White, & Ágústsdóttir, 1991	Infant Temperament, family dynamics, social status.	23 families in Iceland having first baby and 27 families having second child. Data collected in third trimester of pregnancy and when infant was 8 to 9 months. FDM, Revised Infant Temperament Questionnaire (RITQ), Björnsson-Edelstein Scale of Occupational Class.	Mothers perceived decreased role reciprocity. More organized families had more rhythmic infants. No association between family structure and family dynamics or infant temperament. After birth, fathers saw more role reciprocity but mothers saw more Individuation and Mutuality. Mothers of second infant had greater Individuation.
Tomlinson, White, & Wilson, 1990	Family structure (married; nonmarried), social status, dimensions of family dynamics.	Convenient quota sample (first and second baby) of 160 women and 65 of their partners. FDM	Couples who were married and had higher social status had more positive family dynamics (Individuation, Stability, Flexibility, Mutuality, and Communication).
Wilson, Hall, & White, 1994	Family functioning, infant temperament.	99 families in Denmark studied during last trimester and again when child was 8-9 months. FDM RITQ	Both mothers and fathers reported increase in Role Conflict from time 1-2. Mothers reported increased Rigidity and fathers, Isolation. Mothers reported more conflict in roles, while fathers reported more Enmeshment and Isolation. Families reporting more stability, clearer communication, and more mutuality had more rhythmic infants. Fathers of more difficult babies had a greater increase in Role Conflict.

functioning. Several concepts—hardiness, coherence, flexibility, family bonding, and times/routines—are used to classify family typology. The authors maintain that understanding these family typologies is helpful when diagnosing the family's response to emerging or continuing stressors and planning intervention strategies. Three family typologies have been identified in this model. Regenerative families are characterized by high levels of family hardiness and coherence; resilient families are characterized by high bonding and flexibility; and rhythmic families, by high level of family time and routines and valuing this structure. The authors indicate that regenerative families have a sense of family integrity which facilitates their ability to manage hardships. These families feel in control, are secure in a sense of purpose, are active, and when faced with difficulties are more caring, loyal, and more tolerant of hardships (McCubbin, Thompson, & Pirner, 1986; McCubbin & Thompson, 1987). Rhythmic family types highlight family times and routines to create a predictable pattern of family living; and resilient family types are high in family flexibility and family bonding, which are significant patterns for managing and adapting to stressors.

Currently, this research team has constructed and published several instruments to measure family types: The Family Hardiness Index (FHI), Family Time and Routines Index (FTRI), and Family Coherence (McCubbin & Thompson, 1987, 1991). The measure for Family Hardiness is the instrument that has been used most frequently. Only the FHI will be reviewed in depth, as little or no research was found in the 5-year literature review for the other instruments. Family Times and Routines is a 30-item scale with eight subscales (internal reliability of .88). It has been used in the original studies undertaken by the research team (McCubbin, McCubbin, & Thompson, 1987a, 1987b; McCubbin & Thompson, 1991). Family coherence is measured by a four-item Coherence scale which measures families' appraisal skills to manage life stressors. Internal reliability was .71 in the original studies, and it correlated .80 with the Family Crisis Orientated Personal Evaluation Scales (FCOPES). The authors have developed 14-item scales for Family Flexibility and Bonding, and have reported use of short versions of these scales (seven items each) in one series of studies (McCubbin, Thompson, Pirner, & McCubbin, 1988). Family hardiness is based on the concept of individual hardiness developed by Kobasa (1979). Individual hardiness encompasses both cognitive and behavioral aspects of personality that act as a stress mediator. Individual hardiness consists of commitment, challenge, and control. In this conceptualization, commitment is a sense of meaningfulness of life, challenge is a belief that change is normal in life and brings growth opportunities, and control is a belief that the individual influences the events in one's life. Persons with high hardiness were said to be assertive and decisive. Persons low in hardiness were more passive in responding to life's stressors.

FHI INSTRUMENT DESCRIPTION

The FHI is a 20-item instrument comprising four subscales based on Kobasa's three concepts of individual hardiness: (1) Coorientated commitment is a scale with nine items measuring the family's ability to work together to manage difficulties. (2) Confidence is a scale with four items measuring the family's sense of being able to plan ahead. (3) Challenge is a scale with five items measuring the family's innovation, active approach to experiencing new things, and willingness to learn. (4) Control is a three-item scale measuring the family's sense of being in control. Family hardiness was developed to adapt hardiness to the family unit. Items reflect a "we" rather than an "I" orientation. The instrument can be completed in 5 minutes. No information is available on use by children.

Scoring. A score for family hardiness is obtained by summing the items in the scale. The FHI has a 4-choice response format. False=0, Mostly False=1, Mostly True=2, True=3, NA=0. Most research reports a total FHI score, but subscale scores can also be tabulated (see Table 2.3). Scores for Total FHI range from 0 to 60. Negative items are reversed. No normative data are available. Raw scores, percentages, means, and standard deviations are, however, reported for a sample of 304 middle-class white families. Recently the author has created family hardiness scores by combining parent data. Mother's and father's hardiness scores were classified as either high or low. Then a 4-cell typology was created where families could have parents both in the high category, both in the low category, or father high/mother low or father low/mother high.

Sample Items.

Coorientated commitment:

We have a sense of being strong even when we face big problems.
We work together to solve problems.
We strive together and help each other no matter what.
We listen to each other's problems, hurts, and fears.

Confidence:

We do not feel we can survive if another problem hits us.
Life seems dull and meaningless.
Our work and efforts are not appreciated no matter how hard we try and work.

Challenge:

Being active and learning new things are encouraged.
We seem to encourage each other to try new things and experiences.
We tend to do the same thing over and over ... it is boring.

Control:

> Most of the unhappy things that happen to us are mainly due to bad luck.
> Trouble results from mistakes we make.

PSYCHOMETRIC PROPERTIES

Reliability

Internal Consistency. The total FHI reliability for the original study was .82 with subscale reliabilities of .73 to .82. Subsequent studies report .73 (Carey, Oberst, McCubbin, & Hughes, 1991) and .80 reliabilities (Failla & Jones, 1991) for total FHI, and subscale reliabilities from .49 to .77 (Failla & Jones, 1991).

Test–Retest Reliability. One-month test-retest using two members of families dealing with a high-technology chronic illness was .94.

Inter-Rater Reliability. Not applicable.

Validity

Content Validity. None reported.

Construct Validity. Factor analysis reported for 20 items yielded four predicted factors with item loadings of .51 or above. Current analysis suggests a three-factor structure may be a better fit (M. McCubbin, personal communication, August 1993). All data on factor structure and factor loadings, total item pool, the amount of variance explained, and the eigenvalues are available from the authors.

Concurrent Validity. The original study (McCubbin, McCubbin, & Thompson, 1987) reported correlations with FACES II (r=.22), Family Time and Routines (r=.23), and quality of life scales from r=.15 to r=.20. In addition, Trivette, Dunst, Deal, Hammer, and Propst (1990) found their Family Functioning Style Scale correlated with the total FHI at r=.67 and with the individual scales at r=.60, r=.55, r=.51, and r=.25.

Predictive Validity. Family Hardiness over the life cycle is reported for original data. Family Hardiness dips to its lowest at the couple stage of development and peaks at pre- and school-age stage, with a decline at the adolescent-launching stages and an increase at the retirement stage.

CROSS-CULTURAL USES, GENDER SENSITIVITY, AND VARIANT FAMILY STRUCTURES

None reported but work is in progress with African-American families.

SUMMARY OF STUDIES USING THE FHI

Only a few published studies have used the FHI. One group of researchers has studied several outcomes in a variety of samples of cancer patients. Others have looked at satisfaction regarding family functioning and depression. In each of these studies family hardiness predicted psychosocial outcomes. For a summary of studies using the FHI see Table 2.3.

CRITIQUE SUMMARY

The Family Hardiness Index is a fairly new instrument that has been proposed to measure a buffering or mediating family function variable. The conceptual foundation is built on the better established individual hardiness concept. Preliminary information on the FHI is very promising. Although the original factor analysis identified four dimensions with items loading at .50 or better, recent analysis suggests a three-factor solution may be optimal. The internal consistency reliabilities for the total Hardiness Index are strong, but Failla and Jones's (1991) study reported unacceptable reliabilities for the Challenge and Control subscales. Additional psychometric studies are needed. One strength of the FHI is its place in the larger Resiliency Model of Family Stress Adjustment and Adaptation. In the studies conducted using the FHI, the instrument has frequently explained a substantial amount of the variance in a variety of health outcomes. The instrument is easily administered (5 minutes), which may make it more attractive. Both the instrument and the larger model may be useful to many nurse researchers.

SOURCE

Instruments information, scoring guides, and information from original studies are published in *Family Assessment Inventories for Research and Practice*. Copies of instruments are available from the UW Family Stress and Coping Project, 1300 Linden Drive, Room 147 Home Economics Building, University of Wisconsin-Madison, Madison, Wisconsin 53706. Telephone: (608) 262-5070.

FAMILY FUNCTIONING SCALE (FFS)

History

This instrument was developed in the mid-1980s by Bloom (Bloom, 1985; Bloom & Lipetz, 1987) at the Center for Family Studies at the University of Colorado. This work was undertaken to develop a comprehensive instrument addressing the domains of family function with the fewest possible number of items. A series of four studies examined the addition of items from four established instruments (FES, FCQS, FACES, and FAM). Each subsequent study added items from one of these instruments, yielding a final 75-item instrument. In the first study, items from the FES and Family-Concept Q-Sort (FCQS) were administered in one questionnaire ($n=269$). The response format was standardized in a 4-choice format. This choice was made because neither the True-False of the FES nor the 9-point FCQS format was deemed optimal. The 4-choice option allowed analysis not possible with the true-false format. It also decreased the difficult discrimination needed in a 9-choice format. Cluster analysis of the FES items identified 10 scales with five items, a reduction from the original FES instrument, which had nine items per scale (from 90 to 50 items) (see "Other Data," p. 37). Cluster analysis of the FCQS items yielded five scales, three of which were redundant ($r=.80$) with the FES scale. The addition of the 10 items (2 scales) from the FCQS resulted in a 60-item instrument. In the second study ($n=320$) the 60-item instrument from study 1 and the 111-item FACES I were administered. This study provided replication data for study 1 scales. Cluster analysis also yielded nine clusters of variables for FACES items. One Study 1 cluster was eliminated; two study 2 clusters were combined with a study 1 cluster; and two study 2 clusters were combined. The third study ($n=212$) used the same process, administering the study 2 composite instrument with the FAM. Parallel analysis identified no new dimension of family functioning. Several items from the FAM, however, were added to the control and sociability scales. The Independence and Achievement Orientation scales had consistently low reliabilities and were deleted. The five items with the highest loading were retained for each scale. The final revised instrument had 15 scales with five items each, seven adapted mainly from the FES, two from the FCQS, and six from FACES I. The scales included Cohesion, Expressiveness, Conflict, Intellectual-Culture Orientation, Active-Recreational Orientation, Religious emphasis, Organization, Family Sociability, External Locus of Control, Family Idealization, Disengagement, Demographic Family Style, Laissez-Faire Family Style, Authoritarian Family Style, and Enmeshment. The fourth study addressed validity (see below). A second series of two studies for scale development has recently been conducted (Bloom & Naar, in press).

With data from these studies, the idealized families are characterized by high Cohesion and Expressiveness, very little Conflict, a high Active-Recreational Orientation, high Sociability, an internal Locus of Control, a sense of engagement with one another, a Democratic family style, and an absence of laissez-faire approach to life. The last revision of the factor structure was reported in 1994.

Table 2.3. Selected Studies Using Family Hardiness Index (FHI)

Author's citation	Variables	Samples/measures	Major findings
Carey, Oberst, McCubbin, & Hughes, 1991	Time and difficulty associated with caregiving tasks, caregiver appraisal, caregiver burden, hardiness.	49 family caregivers of patients receiving chemotherapy. Caregiving Burden Scale, Appraisal of Caregiving Scale, FHI	50% of the negative appraisal of caregiving explained by family hardiness, caregiver burden, and caregiver health.
Dunkin, Holzwarth, & Stratton, 1993	Hardships, strengths of families, occupation, gender, family structure, education, residence (rural/nonrural).	206 attendees at Farm Union Meeting in rural setting. FHI, Demographic Form	NSD found in hardiness by family type, age, gender, occupation. Greater control was evident in families where spouse was retired. The more urban groups were hardier.
Failla & Jones, 1991	Family stress, family hardiness, coping, support, satisfaction with family functioning.	Convenience sample of 57 mothers of developmentally delayed children. FFFS, Family Hardiness (FH), Coping Health Inventory for parents (CHIP), Norbeck Social Support	Discrepancy score (FFFS) of family satisfaction predicted by FH, Support, parental age, and family stressors ($R^2=.42$).
Faux & Ford-Gilboe, 1993	Family functioning, hardiness, quality of life.	15-month study of 101 developmentally disabled adults. FFFS, FAPGAR, FHI, and Quality of Life (QOL) Scales	Family functioning scales moderately related ($r=.42$ to $r=.48$); only FHI related to QOL ($r=.57$).
Ladewig, Jesse, & Strickland, 1992	Hardiness, depression, strain, family coping.	49 mothers of children held hostage by 2 gunmen in elementary school interviewed 2 weeks and 4 months after episode. FHI	Family hardiness and coping had more impact on depression at 4 months than 2 weeks. Personal Confidence, social and spiritual support also positively related to outcome.
Munkres, Oberst, & Hughes, 1992	Symptoms, appraisal of illness, self-care burden, initial and recurring cancer, family hardiness.	60 subjects (initial cancer=28, recurrent=32) receiving chemotherapy. Modified Symptom Distress Scale, FHI, appraisal of illness, Profile of Mood states.	Individuals with recurrent cancer had higher symptom distress and self-care burden. NSD in mood scales between groups. FHI not predictive of appraisal or symptoms. Different nursing interventions by group suggested.
Oberst, Hughes, Chang, & McCubbin, 1991	Self-care burden (SCB), stress appraisal, mood, fatigue.	72 adults with cancer receiving radiotherapy in treatment for 4 weeks. Modified Symptom Distress Scale, FHI, appraisal of illness, Profile of Mood states.	Fatigue most distressing symptom. Administration of medication most difficult. Symptom distress predicts SCB; SCB and Hardiness best predictor of appraisal score. Appraisal, symptom distress, Family Hardiness, and SCB explained 55% of variance in affective mood scores.

OVERVIEW OF THE MODEL

Based on systems theory, the concepts included in this model were generated from the analysis of the instruments addressed. Bloom (1985) assumes that well-known instruments represent the concepts of interest in measuring family functioning. The analysis carried out in the original series of four studies identified above is compared to a 'grounded theory' approach of theory development. Grounded theory is based upon systematically obtained and analyzed data. This approach identified concepts both unique to the instruments and concepts in common. Bloom (1985) indicates that the concepts can be categorized in Moos's three overall dimensions, although he adapts the labels: Relationship dimensions, Value dimensions, System Maintenance. A second series of psychometric analysis has recently been carried out on a series of two additional studies by Bloom and Naar (in press). Several alternative items were tested to determine if select item revision improved factor reliabilities and item loadings. The testing of revised items in each of the studies resulted in fairly minor changes and relatively small improvements in the psychometric properties of the factor scores themselves.

FAMILY FUNCTIONING TOOL DESCRIPTION

This is a 75-item Likert-type instrument composed of 15 scales in 4-choice response format. As this instrument is a "hybrid" of four other instruments, it can be assumed that the reading level is about the same as the parent instruments (about 7th-grade reading level or 10–12 years old).

PSYCHOMETRIC PROPERTIES

Initial psychometric analysis was carried out in the original series of four studies (Bloom, 1985) (see history). A recent analysis (Bloom & Naar, in press) of revised factors suggests that factor scores are highly reliable as well as stable over time. Additional information regarding other psychometric aspects of the scales not reported here (including scale score norms) is available from the author.

Reliability

Internal Consistency. All scales retained in the original studies had acceptable reliabilities except the Disengagement scale, which had a low reliability in study 3 but not 2. Scales (Independence and Achievement Orientation) that had consistently low reliabilities over three studies were deleted (Bloom,

Table 2.4. Selected Studies Using Family Functioning Survey (FFS)

Author's citation	Variables	Samples/measures	Major findings
Hampson & Beavers, 1987	Sex differences in perceptions of family functioning.	Sample of 90 undergraduate students were administered several questionnaires. FFS, Self-Report Family Inventory, demographic questionnaire.	Women perceived greater affection and positive emotionality in their families (SFI). Women rated families more cohesive on both scales. On the FFS, women indicated higher Intellectual/Cultural Orientation and lower Enmeshment. In general, the relationships of positive emotional expression and other dimensions of family functioning were stronger in women.
Hulsey, Sexton, & Nash, 1992	Occurrence of childhood sexual abuse; subjects' perceptions of the nature of their childhood families.	55 adult women who had experienced sexual abuse before the age of 17 and 49 nonabused women. FFS (asked to respond as it pertained to the family in which they lived when they were 12 years old).	Abused subjects recalled significantly different family environment. They had families that were isolative, rigidly ruled with authoritarian style, and lacked member autonomy. Abused and nonabused women differed significantly on the following scales: Control; Authoritarian style; Disengagement, Religious Emphasis, Cohesion, Intellectual/Cultural emphasis, and Family Sociability.
Penick & Jepsen, 1992	Family functioning, adolescent career aspirations, SES, gender, and educational achievement.	Cross-sectional survey of 215 11th-grade students and their parents. FFS, Career Planning Involvement Scale (Assessment of Career Development), Vocational Identity Scale.	Dimensions of family functioning were more frequent and stronger predictors of career development than gender, SES, and educational achievement.
Tubman, 1991	Families dealing with problem drinking, family functioning, child characteristics, parent characteristics.	26 families with drinking problem and 27 controls recruited from the general community (data obtained from parents and at least one child). Alcohol Dependence Scale, FFS, Kansas Marital Satisfaction Scale	Comparison of families (groups based on fathers' number of alcohol dependence symptoms) yielded potent differences in marital quality, family functioning, maternal depression, social support, and child behavior problems. Has implications for identification and further assessment of these families at risk.

1985). Reliability of the Disengagement scale was not improved dramatically (-.68) in the revision of the scales (Bloom & Naar, in press).

Test–Retest Reliability. Not reported.

Inter-Rater Reliability. Not applicable.

Validity

Construct Validity. See history. In addition, a fourth study used factor analysis with varimax rotation to examine the factor structure. Results were similar to those from study 3 but not identical. The scales from Study 3 were retained (Bloom, 1985).

Concurrent Validity. Ellwood and Stoberg (1991) used five of the factors to assess family impact on divorce adjustment. Positive communication and supportive family relationships were related to Cohesion and Democratic Family Style whereas poor family relationships and communication styles were related to Conflict or Laissez-Faire Style.

Discriminant Validity. A majority of the scales discriminated known groups (intact versus disrupted families). Shean and Lease (1991) found the Enmeshment factor was significantly related to agoraphobic anxiety. Nash, Hulsey, Sexton, Harralson, and Lambert (1993) found scores on eight of the nine factors differentiated women who had been sexually abused from those who had not. Composite scores differentiated women with significant psychopathology from a control group.

Other. Stark, Humphrey, Cook, and Lewis (1990) developed a 12-scale children's version of the items for a study of 51 schoolchildren. The scales differentiated the depressed or anxious children from those who were not, and correctly classified two thirds of children into these categories based solely on their family scores.

Additional Data. Bloom and Naar's (in press) second-order factor analysis yielded three potential domains. The first addressed adequacy of family functioning; the second, family social relationships; and the third, a type of well-organized and close-knit family with relatively little flexibility or spontaneity.

CROSS-CULTURAL USES, GENDER SENSITIVITY, AND VARIANT FAMILY STRUCTURES

None reported. See cross-cultural sections of the FES, FACES, and FAM. It is expected that this instrument would function in a like manner.

SUMMARY OF STUDIES USING THE FFS

The FFS has been used to explore the relationship of family functioning to a variety of issues (career choices, abused families, alcoholism, gender differences). It has not been used in nursing research. Several of the parent instruments, however, are well known to nursing scholars. A summary of studies using the the FFS are found in Table 2.4.

CRITIQUE SUMMARY

This 75-item instrument is shorter and broader than its parent instruments. Its unique development holds promise for capturing concepts of interest to family scholars. The psychometrics are as strong as those of the original instruments. The 4-choice format has advantages over the 2-choice FES. The tool is relatively new, but its origins may accelerate its use once it is better known in the nursing community.

SOURCE

Dr. B.L. Bloom, Department of Psychology, University of Colorado, Boulder, CO *(Revisions of the Self-Report Measure of Family Functioning* [Technical Report Number 2]). Note: Researchers who are interested in using this instrument to study family functioning should be aware that the factorial analyses were derived, in part, from copyrighted instruments. Researchers who may wish to use the FFS, either in whole or in part, should obtain prior permission from the original copyright holders.

3

Self-Report Instruments Early in Their Development

Five instruments are early in their development but offer promise as measures of family functioning; Assessment of Strategies in Families (Friedemann, 1991); Family Caregiver Scale (Greenberg, Monson, & Gesino, 1993); Family Functioning Style Scale (Trivette, Dunst, Deal, Hammer, & Propst, 1990); Comprehensive Evaluation of Family Functioning Scale (McLinden, 1990); and the Self-report Inventory (Beavers, Hampson, & Hulgus, 1985). Each of these instruments has been generated through a series of studies but has either limited psychometric data or has been used on a very limited basis in current investigations. Critiques of these instruments do not include tables.

ASSESSMENT OF STRATEGIES IN FAMILIES-EFFECTIVENESS (ASF-E)

History

Friedemann (1991) proposes an instrument that addresses previously identified weaknesses in family functioning instruments, mainly lack of theoretical clarity, applicability to a general population rather than families with specific pathology, and lack of minority representation in instrument development studies. Recent work has focused on item development, content validation, and construct validity (Friedemann, 1991).

Overview of the Model

The theoretical framework of this instrument is based on ecological systems concepts and process. The family is viewed as the pivotal group to which individuals belong. Interactions and changes in the environment are assumed to have an effect on individual and family functioning. Two concepts are central, homeostasis and morphogenesis. The first focuses on family stability, and the second on family change. Each family is assumed to have a stable core of traditions and values, as well as the necessary flexibility to change as the need arises. While homeostatic and morphogenic family functioning are considered unique dimensions, the author assumes that both are essential for system survival and that the two dimensions may be related to some extent. A third dimension of importance, support-seeking behaviors at the family level, was identified as a concept to be evaluated independently in measuring family functioning.

ASF-E INSTRUMENT DESCRIPTION

A 15-item self-report instrument was developed. Each item consisted of three statements that express outcomes of family functioning. The respondents are asked to pick the statement that best expresses their family's reality. The statements are assigned scores based on level of functioning, with Level 1 being the lowest and level 3 the highest. The Level 3 family functioning is defined as the level necessary for families to maintain themselves and grow over time.

Scoring. Subscale scores were obtained by summing the scores of items on each subscale. The total score is the sum of the three subscale scores (homeostasis, morphogenesis, and support).

Sample Items. (dimensions represented/level of statement)

Our family is generally happy (homeostasis/Level 3).

Everyone in our family is as helpful as possible so that the work gets done (homeostasis/Level 3).

Our neighborhood is bad and we have to protect ourselves from what's going on out there (morphogenesis/Level 1).

If we have a problem with organizations like the schools or the workplace, we fight for our rights (morphogenesis/Level 2).

We don't tell family problems to friends (external support/Level 1).

PSYCHOMETRIC PROPERTIES

Reliability

Internal Consistency. Cronbach's alpha for the total scale and subscales ranged from .60 to .84. The only value below .70 was that for the support scale at .60.

Validity

Content Validity. Initially, 40 items were generated from the literature, clinical experience, and interviews of family clinicians. A group of 14 clinicians, nurses, social workers, and clinical psychologists created the initial items and assigned effectiveness levels. Statements had to reach consensus to remain in the preliminary instrument. Subsequently, a panel of five therapists independently rated the level of functioning of each statement; 100% agreement was the criterion for inclusion. Twelve items were reworded and retested. The 40-item questionnaire was administered to 622 adults. A combination of convenient and purposive sampling was used to obtain diversity in the sample on the domains of family composition (across life span); single and dual parent households; and race.

Construct Validity. Factor analysis with varimax rotation was used to investigate the 40-item questionnaire. Four distinct factors with eigenvalues above 1.0 were identified. The first was a System Homeostasis factor, and the second, a System Morphogenesis (involvement with the community) factor. The third factor reflected morphogenesis on the personal level (individual), and the fourth addressed support. The items with the highest loadings were selected for the final instrument (15 items), and a second factor analysis was conducted. The four-factor solution was duplicated. The two morphogenesis factors were combined for a single morphogenesis subscore. The resulting three subscales were consistent with conceptual underpinnings.

Discriminant Validity. In the initial studies this instrument discriminated between clinical and community families and those who reported symptoms and those who did not ($p<.001$).

CROSS-CULTURAL USES, GENDER SENSITIVITY, AND VARIANT FAMILY STRUCTURES

Two studies are currently in progress, one with 140 substance-abusing families from the African-American community (Friedemann, in press) and one with 50 African-Americans without identified problems. The instrument has been translated into German. Selected scales in the translated version have low reliabilities. The author proposes that the literal translation may not capture the concept of interest in a differing culture (personal communication, 1993).

CRITIQUE SUMMARY

This instrument addresses some of the deficiencies identified by family scholars in previous instrument critique. It has a clear conceptual basis, addresses families in general, addresses the relationship of the family with the larger society, and uses a diverse sample for instrument development. Initial psychometric analysis supports both the factor structure and the reliability of the scales (with the exception of support). The author plans extensive testing with large samples and continued psychometric development. Studies in progress include families with an unemployed member, caregivers of families with elders, and a longitudinal study of individuals with substance-abuse behaviors.

SOURCE

Marie-Luise Friedemann, R.N., Ph.D., Assistant Professor, College of Nursing, Wayne State University, 5557 Cass Avenue, Detroit, Michigan, (313) 577-4092.

COMPREHENSIVE EVALUATION OF FAMILY FUNCTIONING (CEFF)

History

This instrument addresses family functioning in families with special needs children. The author indicates that data on the specific ways in which parents of handicapped children are affected by the presence of this child in their family can be useful to professionals working with the parent. The instrument was designed to measure both the frequency with which various situations or feelings occur in a family as well as the extent to which parents perceive these situations as problematic (McLinden, 1990).

Overview of the Model

No conceptual model is provided.

CEFF INSTRUMENT DESCRIPTION

The CEFF has 51 items organized into seven logically derived subscales: Time Demands, Acceptance, Coping, Social Relationships, Financial, Well-Being, and Sibling Relationships, with subscales having from 2–11 items each. The CEFF has a duel response format to capture both the frequency with which the item occurs and the value of the frequency.

Sample Items.

The demands of caring for my child with special needs make it difficult for me to find time for myself (time demands).

The demands of caring for our child with special needs limit the amount of time we can spend with family and friends (social relationships).

My child with special needs makes progress in his/her development (acceptance).

Scoring. The instrument uses a Likert-type format for the frequency dimension. Frequency was indicated as occurring from 1 (never occurs) to 5 (always occurs). The problem scale was dichotomous (1 = yes; 0 = no). Negatively worded items were recoded so that higher scores reflect greater negative impact.

PSYCHOMETRIC PROPERTIES

The study data were obtained from 32 mothers and 32 fathers who have a child with a disability.

Reliability

No reliability data are presented.

Validity

No content, construct, or concurrent validity information is supplied.

Discriminant Validity. Although there was no difference between mothers and fathers on FACES and the Family Strengths instruments, three subscales of the CEFF were significantly different: Time Demands, Coping, and Well-Being.

CRITIQUE SUMMARY

Although specifics on the development of this instrument are lacking and psychometric development is crucial, data from this study would suggest a family functioning instrument that is specific to the needs of the identified population may generate the most useful information for clinicians intervening with these families.

SOURCE

Stacey E. McLinden, Ph.D., University of Wisconsin-Milwaukee, Milwaukee, Wisconsin.

UNIVERSITY OF WISCONSIN FAMILY ASSESS-MENT CAREGIVER SCALE (UW-FACS)

History

The authors indicate that family gerontologists have long proposed that caring for an elderly relative affects everyone in the family. They found, however, that most of the family functioning instruments were created to reflect families with young children. They concluded that a major gap in family gerontology was the lack of a reliable and valid measure assessing family functioning with a caregiving component (Greenberg et al., 1993).

Overview of the Model

The proposed instrument was based on a systems model. The research team generated five dimensions of family functioning critical to the family system with caregiver responsibilities for a member of the family system. Review of the literature and expert consultation conceptualized these domains as: Validation, Family of Origin, Problem Solving, Roles, and Boundaries. The first of these domains, Validation, refers to family behaviors that reflect the importance of the caregiver activities. Items reflect acknowledgment, support, and appreciation of the primary caregiver's role in the family. The second construct, Family of Origin, reflects the past history of the relationship between the caregiver and recipient. The third, Problem Solving, reflects the family's skill in problem solving around caregiving issues. The Role dimension reflects the degree to which caregiving tasks are clearly delineated and shared within the family. Finally, the Boundary dimension reflects the inclusion or exclusion of family members in caregiving tasks and the family's willingness to seek help outside the family when needed. The instrument was designed to illuminate both family strengths and vulnerabilities.

UW-FACS Instrument Description

This is a 21-item instrument.

Sample Items.

While growing up, I never seemed able to please my parents (Family of Origin).
Everyone in my family knows what is expected of them in helping care for my parent (Roles).
When we have problems with my parent's care, we are pretty good at coming up with different ways to solve them (Problem Solving).
Family members seem to understand the difficulties of caring for my parent (Validation).

Scoring.
Respondents are asked to indicate agreement on a 5-point Likert-type scale with 1 = strongly disagree to 5=strongly agree. In computing subscale scores, items are recoded so that a high score reflects a functional caregiving family system. The total UW-FACS score is the sum of the values on the 21 items.

PSYCHOMETRIC PROPERTIES

Existing instruments were examined to determine viable items for adaptation for families with elderly members. In addition, three family therapists with expertise in aging were recruited to develop construct-specific items. Ninety-five items were created for initial scale development.

Reliability

Internal Consistency. The Cronbach alphas for the subscales ranged from .56 to .85, with Family of Origin and Boundaries having alphas of .56 and .68, respectively; the rest of the reliabilities were above .70. The Cronbach alpha for the total score was .85.

Validity

Content Validity. Ten family gerontologists evaluated the content validity of each item and classified each item on a 7- point functional scale, with 1 = highly dysfunctional family behavior and 7 = highly functional family behavior. These raters were used to determine if there was consensus on the classification of items as representing functional or dysfunctional family patterns. High consensus existed. Items were retained to achieve a balance between questions that reflected highly dysfunctional and highly functional family behavior.

Construct Validity. None reported.

Concurrent Validity. Clinicians who had clients on their case load for over 6 months were asked to rate the family on the same 7-point scale (1=highly dysfunctional caregiving situation to 7=highly functional caregiving situation) on the following dimensions: family's overall functioning as a caregiving system to the frail elderly member; level of stress the family was experiencing; the primary caregiver's mental health; the family's organizational skill to accomplish caregiving tasks and family conflict. The screeners also assessed if there was any risk of abuse. The total FACS score was significantly correlated with clinicians' rating of family functioning (r=.36). Correlations of subscale scores with the clinical ratings ranged from .19 to .38. In addition, the total FACS score was negatively related to caregiver stress (r=-.21), with families who scored higher in family functioning having lower levels of family stress. It was also related to caregiver's mental health (r=.27) and to the clinical rating scales (r=.12 to r=.30). Validity coefficients were acceptable. The stringent content validity methods, the statistically significant nature of the validity coefficients, and the similar pattern across concurrent findings are cited by the authors as supporting the validity of the FACS.

CRITIQUE SUMMARY

Increasing numbers of families will have older members and will be facing caregiver issues. Scholars have proposed that the standard of care for frail elderly include an evaluation of family functioning. This new instrument may be an effective way to highlight family strengths and vulnerabilities. The work to date is preliminary but solid. The authors recommend that the scales with the low reliabilities (Boundaries and Family of Origin) not be used separately until either further studies with larger samples give some evidence of subscale reliability or until scale revision is carried out. Further, the creators of this instrument indicate the populations used to date to develop the instrument are white, predominantly adult daughters or wives. These subjects were fairly well educated and lived in an urban area with a large ethnic support network. Further psychometric evidence is needed, but the instrument may be very helpful in this specific and growing population.

SOURCE

Jan Greenberg, Ph.D., Todd Monson, M.P.H., and Jack Gesino, D.S.W., School of Social Work, University of Wisconsin, Madison, WI 53706.

FAMILY FUNCTIONING STYLE SCALE

History

The Family Functioning Style Scale (FFSS) is one of a battery of instruments created to measure the concepts in the Assessment and Intervention Model aimed at enabling and empowering families (Dunst, Trivette, & Deal, 1988). Other instruments measure additional concepts in the model: needs, aspirations, social support, and resources. This work has been developed over the last 10 years by researchers at the Western Carolina Center for Family Infant and Preschool Program. The program of research created instruments specifically for professionals in the early intervention field but useful to a wider audience. The authors propose that these early intervention specialists are being asked to function as "family specialist" and need reliable and valid instruments (Trivette et al., 1990).

Overview of the Model

The theoretical framework of the instrument is based on a systems framework that includes the concepts Family Functioning Style, Needs, Support, Resources, and Helping Behavior. The earlier concepts are thought of as interlocking gears, whereas help-giving behavior is thought of as the mechanism for aligning the gears in a way that makes the other parts of the system work the most efficiently. The model can be described as a dynamic and fluid guide for professions interacting with a family. Family Functioning Style is defined as the family's types of strength/competencies, capabilities, or unique ways of dealing with life events and promoting growth. The instrument was originally developed to measure 13 concepts clustered in three general dimensions: Family-Identity, Information-Sharing, and Coping/Resource. After psychometric studies five factors were identified: Commitment, Cohesion, Communication, Competence, and Coping.

FFSS Instrument Description

A 26-item self-report instrument measures the extent to which an individual(s) believes their family is characterized by different capabilities or strengths. The respondents are asked to respond "To what extent is each of the following statements like your family." In the qualitative component of the instrument, subjects are asked to "write down all things that you consider to be the major strengths of your family." Respondents are urged not to overlook "little things that occur every day which we often take for granted." The instrument can be filled out by individuals or the family unit (no directions were given about how to administer to the family unit). The authors caution that instructions to the family are crucial, as well as clarity about how the results will be used. The instrument is aimed at clinical practice, allowing the clinician to react to the instrument's score to facilitate interactions (Trivette et al., 1990). For example, the clinician could use the instrument to clarify ("you indicated that family members are willing to pitch in and help...in what ways do they do this?") or reinforce positive behavior ("The fact that you communicate so well in your family must really help in dealing with the concerns we talked about earlier").

Scoring. Subjects respond to a 5-point Likert-type scale, which includes choices: "not at all"; "a little"; "sometimes"; "generally"; or "always" like my family. Subscales are obtained by summing item scores.

Sample Items. (dimensions represented)

Spend time together even with busy schedules (Commitment)
Family sticks together no matter the difficulties (Cohesion)
Family members listen to both sides of disagreements (Communication)
Decision making done to benefit entire family (Competence)
Family makes decisions about solving problems (Coping)

PSYCHOMETRIC PROPERTIES

Current work is expanding the preliminary psychometric studies based on a sample of 105 parents of preschool-aged children (Trivette et al., 1990).

Reliability

Internal Consistency. Analysis of the preliminary sample revealed evidence of internal stability. The coefficient alpha and the split-half reliability coefficients for the overall scale were .92. Cronbach's alphas for the subscales were .84 for Commitment, .85 for Cohesion, .79 for Communication, .79 for Competence, and .77 for Coping. No test-retest data were reported.

Validity

Content Validity. None reported.

Construct Validity. A principal components factor analysis using oblique rotation (as authors assumed factors would be interrelated) was conducted. Items loaded .40 or above on five scales: Commitment, Cohesion, Communication, Competence, and Coping.

Concurrent Validity. The FFSS correlated $r=.73$ with the overall Family Hardiness Scale, indicating that the instruments measured similar qualities of family functioning. Subscale correlations ranged from $r=.10$ to $r=.51$.

Predictive Validity. The authors report predictive validity with the Psychological Well-Being Index and the Mastery and Health subscale for the Family Inventory of Resources and Management. Correlations were $r=.47$ for Psychological well-being and $r=.-54$ for Health problems. Higher FFSS scores were related to higher well-being and less family-related health problems.

Cross-Cultural Uses, Gender Sensitivity, and Variant Family Structures

Has been translated into Spanish.

Studies Using the FFSS

Limited literature is available using the FFSS. One study reported reliability and validity data for the instrument (Trivette et al., 1990). In addition, Ahmeduzzaman and Roopnarine (1991) found two of the subscales (Commitment and Communication) correlated positively with fathers' involvement, specifically, caring for their preschoolers.

SOURCE

Dr. Carol Trivette, Center for Family Studies, Western Carolina Center, 3000 Enola Road, Morganton, NC 28655, (704) 438-6447.

THE SELF-REPORT FAMILY INVENTORY (SFI)

History

The Beavers System Model has been under development over a 20-year period at the Timberlawn Foundation, Southwest Family Institute in Dallas, Texas. Initially, the model emerged from observations of families with schizophrenic adolescents (Beavers, Blumberg, Timken, & Weiner, 1965; Lewis, Beavers, Gossett, & Phillips, 1976) and presently also reflects data obtained from a wide range of clinical and nonclinical families and individuals (Beavers & Hampson, 1993). Model development is guided by general systems theory, clinical work with families, and research investigating family systems. The work of Bateson, Jackson, Bowen, and Wynne heavily influenced this model. Three tools have been developed to measure family competence (functioning) and style, and related psychometric development continues. Family intervention utilizing the Beavers Model is also in the process of development (Beavers & Hampson, 1990). Studies in progress indicate considerable utility entailing intervention strategies based on observational and self-report assessment using the Beavers Model (Hampson & Beavers, 1993).

Overview of the Model

Two levels of family functioning are central to this model: Competence and Style. Competence is present in all families, but patterns range from effective to dysfunctional as a family system carries out tasks to organize and manage itself. Understanding competence displayed in a family's response to small tasks relates to larger tasks, such as raising children. Competence assumes egalitarian leadership, strong parental or other adult coalition, and clear generational boundaries. Competent families result in autonomous members, whose behavior reflects trust, clear and direct communication, spontaneous expression of a wide range of feelings, optimism, and the ability to resolve conflict or accept differences.

The second level of family process is functional and behavioral styles of relating and interacting. In competent families, style is dynamic across the family and individual life cycles. The continuum of style ranges from centripetal to centrifugal, the former reflecting members' seeking gratification primarily from within the family and the latter from outside of the family. Rigid centripetal families result in children who have difficulty leaving home, deny conflict or negative feelings, and exhibit more anxiety and depressive behaviors. Rigid centrifugal families display less trust among family members, are wary of expressing affection, more comfortable with angry feelings, and tend to promote emancipation of members before individuation is complete.

When competence and style are placed on horizontal and vertical axes to each other, nine family types emerge. On the horizontal axis, competence ranges linearly from severely dysfunctional to optimal. On the vertical axis, style is displayed as curvilinear with a mixed or flexible midrange position being the most healthy.

The nine family types are: optimal, adequate, midrange centripetal, midrange centrifugal, midrange mixed, borderline, borderline centripetal, borderline centrifugal, and severely dysfunctional families. Based on data collected from 1,847 families, the distribution of families across the nine family types results in a bell-shaped curve. Thus, about 5% of families overall and up to 19% of nonclinical families fall into the optimal range, and 3% overall and 11% of clinical families fall into the severely dysfunctional range. Midrange families comprise 38% of all families, 25% of nonclinical and 31% of clinical families (Beavers & Hampson, 1993).

Although families can be placed into types, Competence is viewed as being on a continuum and Style is seen as dynamic, thus indicating that observable and measurable growth and adaptation in families is possible. Finally, a central concept of the model is that family assessment is most accurate when perceptions are from at least two sources, referred to as the "insider" and "outsider" perspectives (Hampson, Beavers, & Hulgus, 1989). Three tools have been developed to provide data to meet this criterion. The Beavers Interactional Scales of I. Family Competence and II. Family Style and the Self-Report Family Inventory (SFI) (Beavers, Hampson, & Hulgus, 1985, 1990). The interactional scales are reviewed in the section "Other Family Functioning Measures" in this issue.

SFI INSTRUMENT DESCRIPTION

The SFI was derived from concepts on the observational Competence and Style Scales reviewed. The instrument is composed of 36 items designed to record a family member's perception of their family's Health/Competence (19 items), Conflict (12 items), Cohesion (5 items), Directive Leadership (3 items), and Expressiveness (5 items). The SFI is designed for use with the Beavers Interactional Scales to provide both an insider's and outsider's view of family functioning, or a multilevel and multimethod evaluation. Children ages 10 or 11 are able to complete the SFI independently (Beavers & Hampson, 1993).

Scoring. A Likert-type scale ranging from 1 to 5 is used to record a respondent's perception of how well the descriptive item statement fits one's family for the first 34 items. For the last two items respondents are asked to rate their family on a global functioning item and also the level of independence related to conflict. Scores are transferred onto a scoring sheet that identifies those items to be reverse scored. Items are summed for each of the five factors and averaged. The Health factor is doubled and plotted on the Beavers System conceptual map along the Health/Competence dimension.

Sample Items. (Dimension represented)

	Fits our family very well	Fits our family some		Does not fit our family
1. Family members pay attention to each other's feelings.	1	2 3 (Expressiveness)	4	5
2. Our family would rather do things together than with other people.	1	2 3 (Health/Competence) or (Cohesion)	4	5

PSYCHOMETRIC PROPERTIES

Reliability

Inter–Item Reliability. Alpha reliability evidence ranges from .84 to .88 in diverse clinical and nonclinical samples (Beavers, Hampson, & Hulgus, 1990; Green, 1987; Hulgus & Hampson, 1986).

Test–Retest Reliability. Using a sample of 189 respondents at 1- and 3-month follow-ups, adequate test-retest reliability evidence was found. Family Health and Expressiveness correlations were highest (.85 and .81, respectively) with the average correlation for Directive Leadership being .44. All were statistically significant and indicated adequate temporal stability.

Validity

Content Validity. Based on more than 30 years of clinical work and research with a wide range of individual and family functioning, the core constructs of the Beavers Model which the SFI was designed to measure were identified by W. Robert Beavers, his staff at the Southwest Family Institute, and selected family professionals. Forty-four items were designed to comprehensively represent the dimensions of the Beavers Systems.

Construct Validity. Using a 3-point scale to record a family member's rating of how well the item fit one's own family, data have been collected from a number of diverse samples to validate the SFI (Green, 1987). Based on factor analysis of the original 44 items, four factors were revealed: Health, Expressiveness, Leadership, and Style. For the current 36-item version which uses a 5-point scale, serial factor analysis of a data pool representing clinical and nonclinical families supported the factor structure. Serial factor analysis for the 36-item version confirmed the factor structure with loadings all > .50 (Halvorsen, 1991).

Concurrent Validity. The SFI demonstrates good convergence with a number of measures of family functioning, including the Bloom Family Evaluation Scale, Moos' FES, and the McMaster FAD (Beavers, Hampson, & Hulgus, 1990; Hulgus & Hampson, 1986).The evidence of convergence with FACES II and III has been inconsistent (Green, 1987; Beavers, Hampson, & Hulgus, 1990). Statistically significant correlations with the Locke-Wallace ranged from .092 to -.61. Comparison of SFI results with the Beaver's Interactional Scales of Competence and Style using canonical correlation revealed a moderately high correlation of .62 (Beavers, Hampson, & Hulgus, 1990).

Discriminant Validity. Discriminant validity evidence was not found when the SFI was correlated with the State-Trait Anxiety Inventory, as 8 of the 12 correlations ranging from .03 to .49 were significant. In addition, previously rated families on competence were correctly identified by the Health/Competence and Expressiveness factors of the SFI (Beavers, Hampson, & Hulgus, 1990).

Other. Low correlations, ranging from $r=-.14$ to $r=.06$, between the SFI and social desirability (Marlowe-Crowne) were found across three test periods with a sample of 189 individuals (Hulgus & Hampson, 1986).

CROSS-CULTURAL USES, GENDER SENSITIVITY, AND VARIANT FAMILY STRUCTURES

The recent and ongoing research of the developers indicates sensitivity to several issues of concern to family researchers. A recent study on gender differences revealed that males tend to show stronger relationships between Leadership and Competence than do females. Females show a greater relationship between Emotional Expression and Competence, although significant gender differences do not exist on Competence (Beavers, Hampson, & Hulgus, 1990; Hampson & Beavers, 1987). Within families family position has shown to be related to family competence ratings. In better-functioning families, a greater discrepancy between parents' and adolescent (lower) ratings exists when compared to less-competent families where all members tend to report lower functioning more consistently. Fathers in less competent families are also more likely than the adolescent to rate lower competence and cohesion (Beavers, Hampson, & Hulgus, 1990).

Age-of-recall effects on family-of-origin ratings have also been noted. Recall of family competence when age 10 yielded higher ratings than when age 16. Current family ratings fall somewhere in between the other two recall age ratings (Hampson, Hyman, & Beavers, 1994). Finally, recent findings (Kelley, 1992) indicate that the SFI is appropriate for measuring family functioning in family households in which there is only one parent. Finally, the SFI has been used to compare families representing white, black, and Afro-American ethnic groups (Hampson, Beavers, & Hulgus, 1990).

SUMMARY OF STUDIES USING THE SFI

The SFI is a relatively new self-report instrument developed from the Beavers Interactional scales. The few studies reported in the literature are focused on establishing psychometric evidence or focus on family-related research issues such as age-of-recall and perceptive differences by gender. Only one study was found that examined family competence and its relationship to other variables (Sheridan & Green, 1993). This study investigated differences in Family-of-Origin, Competence, and individual characteristics (self-identity, self-esteem, and control) of 55 adult children of alcoholics (ACOAs) compared to 33 non-ACOAs. Results indicated that compared to non-ACOAs, ACOAs had significantly greater family and individual dysfunction.

CRITIQUE SUMMARY

This is a relatively short, easy to administer instrument that can be used with children as young as 9 years of age, making it attractive for research with families with latency-aged children whose perspectives are desired. Although factor analysis has established the five factors of this instrument, overlap of some items among scales exists. The ongoing research related to gender, family position, and age-of-recall perceptions addresses prevalent validity issues in family research. The results provide evidence that researchers need to think about critically: who in the family should report, whether multiple methods of data collection need to be used, and how valid results are in retrospective studies. Although use of the SFI with the Interactional Style Scales is strongly urged, the practicality of this approach is questionable given the resources necessary for this multimethod approach (see Competence and Style Scales reviews, in "Other Family Functioning Measures" in this issue).

SOURCE

Instruments, scoring guides, and interpretive diagrams ($6-$9.00), manual ($57.00), articles ($5.00), and related books ($16-$24.00) are available from: Southwest Family Institute, 12532 Nuestra Drive, Dallas, TX 75230-1718. Telephone: (214) 960-0550.

4

Other Family
Functioning Measures

GENOGRAM

History

The genogram is a visual representation of a family's composition, structure, relationships, and other information over time, typically for three generations. It is analogous to a "family tree" in format. Initially based on an anthropological instrument, the genogram has been undergoing development since the 1970s for use by professionals, including nurses, working with families.

Overview of the Genogram

The theoretical basis of the genogram is family systems theory, particularly the theory of Murray Bowen, and developmental theory (Gerson & McGoldrick, 1985). The genogram is a clinical tool to collect, organize, assess, plan, and facilitate intervention, evaluate client outcome, and train health care personnel in family-focused practice (Shellenberger, Shurden, & Treadwell, 1988). The genogram can present considerable and complex family data on a one-page diagram that lends itself to interpretation/assessment based on family systems theories. In this regard it provides qualitative data on family functioning dimensions such as Communication, Relationship Patterns, and Family Balance/Imbalance (Darkenwald & Silvestri, 1992). In addition, this tool can be used to collect other data important to a comprehensive family assessment (Visscher & Clore, 1992), such as the impact of stressor events on health care outcomes (Beach, Nagy, Tucker, & Utz, 1988) and patterns of substance abuse or family violence (Bennett, 1992; Sproul & Gallagher, 1982).

Genograms have also been applied to intervention with individuals and families. They are reported to be useful in working with the elderly, as they provide a framework for the client to organize and reconsider life events (Erlanger, 1990; Gerson & McGoldrick, 1985; Herth, 1989). The genogram has been evaluated for facilitating relationships with clients (Darmsted & Cassell, 1983; Erlanger, 1990; Ingersoll-Dayton & Arndt, 1991; Shellenberger, 1989) with mixed results.

There has been considerable use of the genogram in the training of professionals for knowledge and skills in various areas. For example, genograms have been used to sensitize students to cultural differences in families by having students compare a personal genogram to those of families with a diverse heritage (Hardy & Laszloffy, 1992; Kelly, 1990). Genograms have been used to interview prospective family practice students (Blossom, 1991), which has resulted in sensitizing students to a family perspective. Teaching the application of family systems theory (Mengel & Mauksch, 1989; Salgado de Bernal, 1990) has also been facilitated by using genograms, frequently by having participants complete a personal genogram and compare it to the type of family genogram with which they will work.

Standardization of the genogram has not occurred, but there have been some attempts to do so reported in the literature (Friedman & Krakauer, 1982; Like, Rogers, & McGoldrick, 1988; Rogers & Durkin, 1984; Rohrbaugh, Rogers, & McGoldrick, 1992). The most comprehensive presentation (Gerson & McGoldrick, 1985) is a text that provides detailed information on the construction of the genogram, including a basic genogram interview format. Interpretation guidelines include family structure, life cycle fit, pattern repetition across generations, life events and family functioning, relational patterns and triangles, family balance and imbalance.

In more recent years variations of the genogram have developed. These include the Time-Line Genogram (Friedman, Rohrbaugh, & Krakauer, 1988), client administered genograms (Rogers & Rohrbaugh, 1991) and computerized development of genograms for clinical and research uses (Chan, Donnan, Chan, & Chow, 1987; Ebell & Heaton, 1988; Gerson, 1984).

Scoring. Not applicable.

Sample Items. The literature reflects variation in the notation of family data for constructing genograms, although there appears to be considerable consensus about basic symbols used and guidelines about placement of information (Gerson & McGoldrick, 1985; Hartman, 1978).

Symbols.   Male: □   Female: ○   Death: ☒

Marriage: □⎯M41⎯○   Divorce: □⎯M41, D50⎯○

Children: List in birth order, beginning with oldest on left:
□⎯⎯⎯⎯⎯⎯⎯○
(14) (10) (7) (1)

Very close relationship: □≡≡○

Conflicted relationship: □∿∿∿○

PSYCHOMETRIC PROPERTIES

The genogram has been in use primarily for clinical practice for over 20 years. The literature reflects considerable use of case examples to present the applications of the genogram. The continued use of the genogram by several disciplines over time provides evidence of face validity. Attempts thus far to establish psychometric evidence have been few and have resulted in conflicting results. In part, the genogram is difficult to evaluate psychometrically. For example, the range of family theories to explain dynamics can result in various explanations of the same genogram (theoretical biases), a factor that does not appear to have been considered in the research to date. Also, there is the phenomenon that different family members have different accounts of the same event (Rashomon effect) (Gerson & McGoldrick, 1985).

Reliability

Inter–Item Reliability. Not applicable.

Test–Retest Reliability. Based on a sample of 11 female patients over a 3-month period, there was a high degree of reliability related to structure, demographics, and life events, as well as similar rates of completion time (Rogers & Holloway, 1990).

Inter-Rater Reliability. In a study to determine if there was agreement about the categories from a genogram that were important in predicting health risks, there was poor agreement about the relative importance of the identified categories (Rohrbaugh, Rogers, & McGoldrick, 1992).

Validity

Content Validity. No available evidence.

Construct Validity. No available evidence.

Concurrent Validity. No available evidence.

Discriminant Validity. No available evidence.

Predictive Validity. The genogram has been shown to provide an average of four times as much family medical information when compared to informal interviews. This study also found that conducting a genogram interview resulted in more client requests for psychosocial counseling and increased identification of family problems such as substance abuse when compared to informal interviews (Rogers & Durkin, 1984). Another study (Rogers & Cohn, 1987) found that the genogram collected more information about structure, life events, repetitive illness, and family relationships, but there were no differences on the hypothesized dependent variables of family issues exploration, requests to see other family members, or referrals for counseling or other problems.

There has been some research to evaluate professionally constructed genograms compared to patient constructed genograms and no genogram (Rohrbaugh, Rogers, & McGoldrick, 1992). The results indicated that there were no differences between the groups in relation to increased physician sensitivity to psychosocial issues, impact on patient/physician relationship, or process of clinical care.

The genogram has shown agreement by judges to 7 of 26 relevant data categories available on a genogram that would predict health risks (Rohrbaugh, Rogers, & McGoldrick, 1992). There was poor agreement between judges, however, regarding the relative importance of these categories.

Other Data. Computer applications of the genogram have been developed (Chan et al., 1985; Ebell & Heaton, 1988; Gerson, 1984; Gerson & McGoldrick, 1985). These programs are intended for use in clinical practice as well as for family historians or others wanting to record personal family data. Computer applications make it easy to update genograms and search for particular types of data, particularly in families that are complex.

CROSS-CULTURAL USES, GENDER SENSITIVITY, AND VARIANT FAMILY STRUCTURES

The genogram has been used with reported success in identifying women's issues for teaching purposes (Howe, 1990). It has been used cross-culturally (Salgado de Bernal, 1990), and is recognized by professionals in family therapy as having sensitivity to cross-cultural and variant family structures (Boyd-Franklin, 1989; McGoldrick, Pearce, & Giordano, 1982).

SUMMARY OF STUDIES USING GENOGRAMS

In addition to the training of health care professionals, genograms have been applied to a number of populations, and problems to which nurses respond. These include substance abuse, suicide, persons in crises, and the elderly. For a summary of studies using genograms see Table 4.1.

CRITIQUE SUMMARY

The use of the genogram in the education, training, and continued development of professionals has been the most noteworthy due to attempts to evaluate the effectiveness of this tool. The earlier findings pointed to effectiveness of outcome, but more recent training using the genogram has yielded mixed results, indicating the need for further evaluation of the effectiveness of this approach. The mixed results of existing research may indicate that more recent students have more information of a family systems orientation at the time of training, particularly if it is at the advanced level, such as for physicians. Since the genogram is a graphic or visual representation of complex family data, the use of this tool may be related to individual learning styles, as this body of knowledge has shown that there are variations, with some students learning more through visual data and others through experiential methods, for example. This area has not been explored in the research to date.

The continued use of the genogram in practice provides reason to pursue future research to establish further validity and reliability evidence. Future evaluation of the use of the genogram in practice is critical if it continues to be used. This research should focus on training use as well as clinical applications for assessment of family functioning, client interventions, and client outcomes.

Continued attempts to standardize various aspects of the genogram would be helpful for many reasons. It would assist the research process to establish the psychometric properties of the genogram. It would aid in the cross-disciplinary uses of the tool in both research and clinical practice by promoting a common "language" through standardization.

SOURCE

There is not an identified source to obtain permission, information on current research in progress, or other genogram materials. The text by McGoldrick and Gerson, *Genograms in Family Assessment,* is available from the publisher, W.W. Norton & Company (ISBN 0-393-70002-X for paper; ISBN 0-393-70023-2, clothbound).

MCMASTER STRUCTURED INTERVIEW OF FAMILY FUNCTIONING (MCSIFF)

History

The McSiff is an interview protocol for clinical, research, and teaching purposes. It is based on the theory of the McMaster Model of Family Functioning which originated in the Departments of Psychiatry at McGill and McMaster Universities in Canada during the 1960s and 70s. This research continues at Brown University and Butler Hospital in Providence, Rhode Island. The development of McSiff has emerged from the research, clinical work, and teaching of the McMaster Model. Research to establish adequate psychometric properties is currently in progress.

Table 4.1. Selected Studies Using Genograms

Author's citation	Variables	Samples/measures	Major findings
Arrington, 1991	Art therapy Family therapy	Case study of adolescent inpatients using art therapy model, family history, genogram Kwiatkowska's structured art evaluation	Family dynamics of spousal & sibling subsystems, roles, boundaries, coalitions, scapegoating, myths, & secrets evaluated.
Blossom, 1991	Selection of applicants, interest in families.	43 medical student applicants; personal genogram	Results indicated positive experience that impacted perception of program and sensitized subjects to family issues.
Erlanger, 1990	Counseling techniques with elderly	Case examples; genogram	Genogram useful to establish relationship with elderly, provides framework for client to deal with past issues, gathers data base information for therapy.
Friedman & Krakauer, 1992	Genogram format compared to outcome	3 groups of students, each using different way to record & interpret family information; time-line genogram, genogram	3 groups equally successful; group using time-line genogram best at recording events linked in time.
Howe, 1990	Training for women's issues	Case example; genogram	Students became less blaming with increased close feelings to mother & more affection expression; increased knowledge of use of genogram in therapy for similar outcome.
Kelly, 1990	Counselor training for cultural attitudes and beliefs	Case example; genogram	Students discovered own cultural background in relation to diverse cultural group content.
Like, Rogers, & McGoldrick, 1988	Systematic use of genogram	Three clinical case studies; genogram	Six information categories of family data described for use in generating and testing clinical hypotheses related to genograms.

Source	Focus	Method	Findings
Mengel & Mauksch, 1989	Health care provider training to work with difficult patients	Description of a 5-phase training curriculum; genogram	Trainees increased knowledge and skill of impact of family dynamics on provision of care for difficult patients by comparing family of origin genogram to those of difficult patients & their families.
Rogers & Cohn, 1984	Outcome of types of screening.	4 physicians and 72 initial visit patients	Genogram collected more data re: family structure, the events, repetitive illness, and family relations; n.s. on exploration of family issues, requests to see other family members, or referral for counseling or other problems.
Rogers & Durkin, 1984	Interview format, genogram outcome	Physicians for first-time patients; genogram	Semistructured versus informal format yielded 4 times more medical information, including family environment information; 60% described family problem & 32% expressed need for counseling with structured but none with informal format.
Rogers & Holloway, 1990	Completion rate and reliability of genogram	11 female patients at 3-month interval; Self-Administered Genogram (SAGE)	Similar completion rates with high degree of reliability re: structure, demographics, and life events.
Rogers & Rohrbaugh, 1991	Impact of genogram on sensitivity to psychosocial issues & doctor/patient relationship	189 patients visiting 5 physicians; Physician-Administered Genogram (PAGE), Self-Administered Genogram (SAGE)	Randomized clinical trial (SAGE, PAGE, no genogram, baseline groups) revealed no differences re: how physicians think about/deal with clinical problems or how patients view visit; for doctors, PAGE more relevant, less complete than SAGE, & required more physician time.
Rogers, Rohrbaugh, & McGoldrick, 1992	Prediction of short-term health outcomes, genograms	6 physicians predicting outcome using three methods for 20 patients; genogram	Prediction of outcomes over 3-month period using genograms no more accurate than using demographics or patient charts.

(Continued)

Table 4.1. Selected Studies Using Genograms *(Continued)*

Author's citation	Variables	Samples/measures	Major findings
Rohrbaugh, Rogers, & McGoldrick, 1992	Genogram information, health risks, professional background	6 physicians & 6 family therapists; genogram	7 of 26 categories of genogram information judged relevant to health risk; poor agreement by judges on what was most important.
Salgado de Bernal, 1990	Construction of genogram questions, impact of subjects, and use	17 Columbian adult psychology students each in pilot & evaluation phases.	(not available)
Shellenberger, 1989	Caregiving needs & stresses	15 elderly subjects and their caregivers; structured interview, family history, genogram	Some subjects viewed caregiver as less involved with subjects than siblings of caregivers; 60% caregivers single, divorced, or widowed; about half held helping or caregiver occupations.
Shellenberger, Shurden, & Treadwell, 1988	Use of personal genogram in training/faculty development	Evaluation of faculty development series using personal genogram.	Unexpected outcome of increased understanding of colleagues in work setting.
Vukov & Eljdupovic, 1991	Family structure & drug addiction	41 Yugoslavian families with/without opiate addicted member; family interview and genogram.	No difference between groups; most families intact at onset of addiction; possible risk factors related to birth order noted.

OVERVIEW OF THE MODEL

The McMaster Model is based on systems, role, and communications theories, and evolved from work with nonclinical families. An important theoretical assumption is that families can report healthy functioning in some dimensions while experiencing difficulties in other(s). The model also is based on the assumption that, "The primary function of today's family unit appears to be that of a laboratory for the social, psychological, and biological development and maintenance of family members" (Epstein, Levin, & Bishop, 1976, p. 1411). In order to represent the complexities of a family, the model identifies six dimensions (structural and organizational properties) of family functioning: Problem Solving, Communication, Roles, Affective Involvement, Affective Responsiveness, and Behavior Control. Each dimension is operationally defined so that both optimal and pathological functioning are clear. Three assessment instruments have been developed based on this model. These are the McMaster Structured Interview for Family Functioning (McSIFF) which is reviewed here, the Clinical Rating Scale (MCRS), and the Family Assessment Device (FAD), also included in this review.

McSIFF INSTRUMENT DESCRIPTION

The interview schedule is designed to be used in conjoint family interviews. The length of an interview varies, typically being $1\frac{1}{2}$-2 hours each for nonclinically trained raters and 1 hour for skilled clinicians trained in the model. There are three versions of the McSIFF, making it applicable to two-parent family households with children, couples only, and single-parent households. Each version is a complete interview schedule designed to assess and rate basic components of the six dimensions of the McMaster Model: Problem Solving, Communication, Roles, Affective Involvement, Affective Responsiveness, Communication, and Behavior Control. The schedule is divided into each of the model dimensions purposely ordered to create clinical interview conditions which ensure a response that most accurately represents the perception of family members. For example, the developers have noted that families respond more openly to content related to Roles, the first dimension, than to Affective Involvement which is the last dimension on the protocol. The first section, orientation to the family, makes statements to the family about the purpose of the interview and solicits their expectations, perceptions, and types of family problems, previous action to address the problems, and the results of any such action. These sections are noted in bold print as major headings. It is expected that a Clinical Rating Scale will also be completed at the end of administering the McSIFF.

In addition to required statements and questions which are presented in bold print, each section contains other possible questions designed to more fully explore the dimension through probing, questioning, and discussion with the family members. The objective is to obtain enough information from the family so that a clear and reasonable rating can be made of the effectiveness of the family in each dimension. Throughout the schedule are blank spaces where responses and other data can be reported as the interview progresses. Such notes are intended to record unusual or unclear responses and detailed content obtained from thorough exploration. These notes are utilized when the interviewer makes final ratings and in coding of data.

Scoring. Interviewers rate the presence or absence of family problems in a specific component of family functioning. These required ratings are noted in boxed areas printed in bold italics throughout the interview schedule. Within each section are subsection ratings related to attributes of the dimension under discussion. For example, under "roles" is a subsection rating the family's ability to meet basic tasks as outlined in the McMaster Model. A "Yes" or "No" and "Comments" format is used to rate both subsection and dimension areas.

Two "coding matrices" also are in the interview schedule. The first is used to question the family about various household tasks and who is involved with carrying out each task. The second matrix notes problems in a range of feelings (pleasure and fear, for example) for each family member.

Sample Items. (subsection/dimension)

1. Interviewer Rating:
   The family is adequately provided
   for in terms of food, shelter,
   transport, clothing, and money   No   Yes

   Comments: _____

   _____

   (Roles subsection)

2. Interviewer's Role Dimension Rating:
   The family is effective in its role
   functioning?   No   Yes

   Comments: _____

   _____

   (Roles Dimension)

PSYCHOMETRIC PROPERTIES

Content Validity

The Family Categories Schema, which resulted from a study of 110 nonclinical families, provided the conceptual framework which was the basis for the McMaster Model (Westley & Epstein, 1969). The dimensions of the McSIFF, which are the same as for the FAD (see "Well-Established Self-Report Instruments" in this issue), were identified from clinical work with families, and research and teaching about families (Epstein, Baldwin, & Bishop, 1983). In the past few years in the course of their clinical work and interdisciplinary training, the developers recognized particular types of questions and a format for interviewing that yielded the best clinical results with most families. These questions were reviewed and added to by researchers with expertise in instrument development resulting in the present McSIFF (Butler/Brown, 1992).

No established psychometric evidence has been reported in the literature for the McSIFF, but research is currently in progress. The McSIFF is currently being used in a longitudinal study of 45 families (Dickstein, Seifer, & Sameroff, 1992) which examines the relationships between maternal mental illness and child outcomes. Based on initial results from data collected by the McSIFF compared to data from the McMaster Family Assessment Device (FAD) and the McMaster Clinical Rating Scale (MCRS), there is evidence of at least moderate concurrent validity.

Preliminary findings from another study utilizing the McSIFF, FAD, and MCRS with 116 families which include a seriously disturbed adolescent member (Bishop & Archambault, 1992) indicate the strongest concurrent validity evidence between the McSIFF and FAD, ranging from .26 for the Behavior Control Scale to .63 for the General Functioning Scale. A third study of depression treatment (Miller & Keitner, 1992) of 60 patients and their families over a 2-year period is currently in progress.

CROSS-CULTURAL USES, GENDER SENSITIVITY, AND VARIANT FAMILY STRUCTURES

The use of the McMaster Model with a broad range of cultural and problem populations worldwide (see McMaster Family Assessment Device in this review) and the preliminary findings of correlation between the McSIFF with the FAD indicate possible use of the McSIFF with a range of family types.

The interview protocol clearly states that all family members are to be involved in providing responses and that any conclusions made by the interviewer are reviewed with the family for accuracy. This points to an underlying assumption that the input of all members is valued and the views of the family unit, not just those of the clinician, focus the intervention with the family. Such values of mutuality and empowerment reflect the current practice literature related to female gender sensitivity and theoretically allow for family values unique to any culture to be recognized.

CRITIQUE SUMMARY

Based on research in progress and the long history of this particular family research group, the McSIFF is a promising instrument for clinical use to assess and measure treatment outcome. It is based on a well-established theoretical model which has been operationalized with a family self-report instrument (FAD) with strong psychometric evidence as well as clinical utility.

The interview schedule is easy to understand and provides clear guidance to the interviewer as to when and how to explore particular areas in more depth. Although it may appear that a novice could apply this protocol, clinical judgment obtained from experience would appear to be necessary, particularly when family members are queried about sensitive emotions. It also seems feasible that administration of the McSIFF would have a treatment effect, which may be another area for further testing.

The comprehensiveness of the protocol is noteworthy and allows for more in-depth assessment of the dimensions presented in the theoretical model than does the FAD. This comprehensiveness requires a face-to-face conjoint family interview, as well as considerably more time than would a written survey format. Research that requires more of an inductive or qualitative understanding of the phenomenon under study may find the McSIFF particularly useful.

SOURCE

The interview schedule in the desired version can be obtained from Butler/ Brown Family Research Group, 345 Blackstone Boulevard, Providence, RI 02906, telephone (401) 456-3700 or -3792. The developers request that users of the McSIFF make raw data available for inclusion in their ongoing studies of the psychometric properties of the instrument. A "Data Coding Form" is available to users to collect the necessary demographic information for families for which the McSIFF is utilized and to report the data from the use of the other McMaster instruments, the Family Assessment Device (FAD), and the McMaster Clinical Rating Scale (MCRS).

BEAVERS INTERACTIONAL SCALES: I.
FAMILY COMPETENCE SCALE

History

See review of the SFI in "Self-Report Instruments Early in Their Development" in this issue.

OVERVIEW OF THE MODEL

See review of the SFI in "Self-Report Instruments Early in Their Development" in this issue.

FAMILY COMPETENCE INSTRUMENT
DESCRIPTION

Ratings of health/competence by a trained observer are made on 13 items, each representing a subscale, based on observation of family interaction. Typically, family interaction focusing on completing a task is videotaped for about 10-15 minutes in a clinical setting. For clinical families, the task question is, "Discuss what you would like to see changed in your family." Normative data were obtained from nonclinical families responding to several questions related to planning a family outing, discussing the meaning of closeness in the family, identifying the most troubling difficulty in the family, and family strengths.

The 13 subscales measured are:

1. Overt Power, ranging from chaos to egalitarian;
2. Parental Coalition, ranging from a parent-child to strong parental;
3. Closeness, ranging from nondistinct to close and distinct;
4. Mythology, ranging from observer-congruent to observer-incongruent;
5. Goal-directed Negotiation, ranging from efficient to inefficient problem solving;
6. Clarity of Expressing, ranging from clear to unclear expression of thoughts and feelings;
7. Responsibility for actions, ranging from regularly to rarely voiced;
8. Permeability, ranging from very open to unreceptive to statements of others;
9. Range of feelings, ranging from open, direct to no expression;
10. Mood and tone, ranging from warm, optimistic, and/or humorous to cynical, hopeless, and/or pessimistic;

11. Unresolved conflict, ranging from severe with impaired functioning to no unresolvable conflict;
12. Empathy, ranging from consistent and empathic to grossly inappropriate responsiveness to feelings;
13. Global health/competence, ranging from least healthy to competent.

Scoring. The first 12 subscales are scored using a 5-point, Likert-type scale, with nine actual anchor points provided by half-point graduations. The Global Health subscale uses a 10-point scale, with 10 being the most pathological. After rating the videotaped segment, scores are reversed on four items, then summed for the first 12 and divided by six. This score is plotted on the Global Health/Competence scale. If the global scores are within one or two points, an accurate rating is assumed. Variance of scores among subscales may indicate relative family strengths and weaknesses. Family scores of 1 or 2 are "optimal"; 3 or 4 "adequate"; 5 or 6, midrange; 7 or 8, borderline; and 9 or 10, severely disturbed.

Sample Items. Dimension represented.
C. Closeness

1	1.5	2	2.5	3	3.5	4	4.5	5

Amorphous, vague & indistinct boundaries among members	Isolation, distancing	Closeness, w/ distinct boundaries among members

Note any invasions (when a family member clearly "speaks for" the thoughts or feelings of another, without invitation):

—invasion(s) observed
—invasion(s) not observed

VI. Global Health-Pathology Scale: Circle the number of the point on the following scale that best describes this family's health or pathology.

10	9	8	7	6	5	4	3	2	1

Most Pathological   Healthiest

PSYCHOMETRIC PROPERTIES

Reliability

Inter-Item Reliability. Alpha reliability has been observed to be .94. Based on factor analysis, only one significant factor has been revealed (Beavers, Hampson, & Hulgus, 1990).

Inter-Rater Reliability. Based on data from 111 raters, reliability coefficients range from .73 for Goal Directed Negotiation to .89 for the Unresolvable Conflict and Global subscales. A .94 coefficient is reported for the average of subscales. Nine of the 13 coefficients are .80 or higher (Beavers, Hampson, & Hulgus, 1990).

Test–Retest Reliability. No available evidence.

Validity

Content Validity. Based on more than 30 years of clinical work and research with a wide range of individual and family functioning, the core constructs for the Competence Scale were identified by W. Robert Beavers, his staff at the Southwest Family Institute, and selected family professionals. No other content validity evidence was available.

Construct Validity. Based on factor analysis, only one significant factor has been revealed (Beavers, Hampson, & Hulgus, 1990).

Concurrent Validity. Based on a normal (N=147) and clinical (N=59) family sample utilizing the Style Scale and Self-Report Scale for the Beavers Model, moderate to high convergence evidence is reported. Health/Competence measured by the SFI and compared to the Competence Scale resulted in a correlation of .62 (p<.01) for clinical families and of .39 (p<.01) for normal families. Correlations with self-reported Conflict, Cohesion, and Expressiveness for clinic families were r=.47, r=.48, and r=.46, respectively (p<.01). Self-reported Communication convergence was low and not statistically significant. Overall, the SFI and Competence Scale show moderately high convergence at .62 (Beavers, Hampson, & Hulgus, 1990; Hampson, Beavers, & Hulgus, 1989).

Discriminant Validity. The Competence Scale was found to differentiate normal (N=149) from clinic (N=61) families in most cases (Beavers, Hampson, & Hulgus, 1990). In a recent study comparing observational and self-report measures from the Beavers, McMaster, and Circumplex Models, the Competence Scale accounted for 84% of the variance in discriminating clinic from nonclinic families (Hampson, Beavers, & Hanks, 1993).

Predictive Validity. Recent findings show that families higher on Competence show greater therapeutic gains than do families rated as having lower levels of Competence (Hampson & Beavers, 1993).

CROSS-CULTURAL USES, GENDER SENSITIVITY, AND VARIANT FAMILY STRUCTURES

In a study of 89 white, 79 black, and 18 Mexican-American families using the Competence Scale and Style Scale, no significant differences on global competence and style were found between groups. Other theoretically important differences supported the hypothesis that ethnic groups reflect stylistic versus competence or health differences.

SUMMARY OF STUDIES USING THE COMPETENCE SCALE

Only two recent studies related to nursing were identified, and both focused on families with a retarded child. One study of 40 families used a structured interview which was videotaped to rate family competence. Based on the ratings, families were divided into four groups: optimal ($n =11$), adequate ($n =11$), midrange ($n =10$), and borderline dysfunctional ($n = 8$). Other data related to structural and power issues, individuation and sibling issues, value issues, and feeling issues were obtained through interview format. The results were compared to competence patterns of higher functioning families without a handicapped child (Lewis, Beavers, Gossett, & Phillips, 1976). Higher functioning families with a retarded child demonstrated greatest competence overall and specifically in Unresolvable Conflict, Mythology, and Responsibility. Families without a handicapped child revealed greatest competencies in Mood and Tone, Mythology, and Parental Coalition. Range of feelings, Empathy, and Permeability were the least adaptive competencies for all families (Beavers, Hampson, Hulgus, & Beavers, 1986).

Another study of 60 families with retarded children was divided into three groups, based on the age of the child (6-8, 12-14, 18-21). Data from trained raters were compared to nonclinical family data. Results indicated that families with the youngest children and those with retarded children who were male were more dysfunctional (Hampson, Hulgus, Beavers, & Beavers, 1988).

CRITIQUE SUMMARY

The use of the Competence Scale in research is labor intensive, as it requires rater training to ensure high reliability, videotaping of live family interaction, and subsequent review time for ratings and/or one-way observation mirror. Rater reliability is critical and must be preestablished with periodic follow-up checks. Training, which takes 8-16 hours, is available through periodic training sessions and workshops offered by the developers. In addition, training tapes can be purchased (Murdock & Beavers, 1992). More psychometric study is needed for the Competence Scale. The scale would appear to have utility for families in therapy to measure treatment outcome. Since the Beavers System Model is concerned with coping and competence, the model would appear to have relevance to nursing scholars concerned with treatment compliance and identification of family competence. The details of the construct selection and development (content validity) need to be made explicit.

SOURCE

See review of SFI in "Self-Report Instruments Early in Their Development" in this issue.

BEAVERS INTERACTIONAL SCALES: II. FAMILY STYLE FOR THE BEAVERS SYSTEM MODEL

History

See "Self-Report Instruments Early in Their Development" in this issue for the SFI.

Overview of the model

See "Self-Report Instruments Early in Their Development" in this issue for the SFI.

FAMILY SCALE INSTRUMENT DESCRIPTION

This 8-item clinician rating scale assesses the interactional style of a family, which ranges from centripetal to centrifugal. Based on videotaped family interactions and responses to the Family Characteristics Inventory and a marital satisfaction instrument, the initial 11-item centripetal/centrifugal scale was developed (Kelsey-Smith & Beavers, 1981). The Style Scale uses the videotaped interaction described in the Beavers Interactional Scales: I. subsection.

Each of the 8 items represents a subscale: Dependency Needs, Style of Adult Conflict, Proximity, Social Presentation, Verbal Expression of Closeness, Aggressive/Assertive Behaviors, Expression of Positive/Negative Feelings, and Global Family Style.

Scoring. Based on rater observations, each item is assigned a value. The first three subscales are reverse scored, added to the sum of the next four items, and averaged to yield an average subscale score. This average is compared to the Global item score. If there is a difference of more than one point, the score should be recalculated. The score is then placed on the provided Beavers Model map.

Sample Item. (Dimension represented).

1. (Dependency Needs).

All families must deal with the dependency needs of members. In this family, the dependency needs of members are:

1	2	3	4	5
discouraged, ignored	sometimes discouraged, sometimes attended			encouraged, alertly attended

PSYCHOMETRIC PROPERTIES

Reliability

Inter-Item Reliability. Alpha reliability has been observed to be .84. Only one significant factor was revealed through factor analysis (Beavers, Hampson, & Hulgus, 1990).

Inter-Rater Reliability. Based on data from 11 raters, reliability coefficients range from .61 for Expressed Closeness to .83 for Proximity and Expression of Positive/Negative Feelings. A .79 coefficient is reported for the average of the subscales. Coefficients for six of the eight subscales are .80 or lower (Beavers, Hampson, & Hulgus, 1990).

Test–Retest Reliability. No available evidence.

Validity

Content Validity. The Beavers Style Scale was developed through observation of 42 families with an adolescent who was a psychiatric inpatient. Based on videotaped family interactions and responses to the Family Characteristics Inventory and a marital satisfaction instrument, the initial 11-item Centripetal/Centrifugal scale was developed (Kelsey-Smith & Beavers, 1981). Continuing work with different types of emotional and behavioral disturbances and clinical observations of binding versus expelling patterns of interaction have furthered the developers' beliefs that the style dimension is inseparable and central to the Beavers Systems model. The conceptual writings of Erikson and Stierlin influenced the selection of concepts and terms of the Style Scale (Beavers et al., 1990). No other content validity evidence was available.

Construct Validity. Based on factor analysis, only one significant factor has been revealed (Beavers, Hampson, & Hulgus, 1990).

Concurrent Validity. Based on a normal (*N*=147) and clinical (*N*=59) family sample utilizing the Competence and Self-Report Scale, moderate and statistically significant correlations were found between the Style Scale and the SFI for the Health/Competence, Conflict, Cohesion, and Expressiveness subscales (Beavers, Hampson, & Hulgus, 1990). When Style Scale scores were compared to SFI scores, there was greater correspondence between adolescents' views of Family Health, Conflict, and Cohesion and those of outside raters than there was between parents' and outside raters' (Hampson, Beavers, & Hulgus, 1989).

Discriminant Validity. No available evidence.

Predictive Validity. Clinic family studies reveal significant difference between Centripetal and Centrifugal families in the distribution of DSM-III-R diagnoses. Centripetal families exhibit significantly more anxiety and unipolar depression compared to Centrifugal families, where more conduct and externalizing disorders are seen (Beavers & Hampson, 1993).

Other Data. No significant relationship was found between the Locke-Wallace Marital Satisfaction Inventory and the Style Scale.

CROSS-CULTURAL USES, GENDER SENSITIVITY, AND VARIANT FAMILY STRUCTURES

In a study of 89 white, 79 black, and 18 Mexican-American families using the Style and Competence Scales, no significant differences on global style and competence were found between groups. Other theoretically important differences supported the hypothesis that ethnic groups reflect stylistic versus competence or health differences. Style is related more to socioeconomic versus ethnic differences, with lower SES associated with more Centrifugal style ratings. The use of the Style Scale with the Competence Scale allows for cultural differences in style, with similar competence levels described without being labelled unhealthy, incompetent, or dysfunctional.

SUMMARY OF STUDIES USING THE
STYLE SCALE

The Style Scale was used in both studies summarized for the Competence Scale, described earlier in this section. In general, extreme style scores were associated with less functional families (Beavers, Hampson, Hulgus, & Beavers, 1986).

CRITIQUE SUMMARY

See earlier in this section, as the same critique applies to the Style Scale as to the Competence Scale. In addition, through the use of this scale, minority families theoretically may be less likely labelled dysfunctional if behaviors different from the norm of the larger society are attributed to stylistic differences where a blend of styles versus rigid adherence to any one is viewed as most functional. Additional research with this focus is needed. More detail describing the selection of constructs (content validity) needs to be published.

SOURCE

See "Self-Report Instruments Early in Their Development" in this issue for the SFI.

Assessment Guides

Another category of instruments, assessment guides, were not reviewed here, but have several strengths the reader may wish to consider (Berkey & Hanson, 1991; Francis & Munjas, 1976; Friedman, 1986; Gilliss, Highley, Roberts, & Martinson, 1989; Holman, 1983; Ross & Cobb, 1990). Generally, these guides are a comprehensive outline of areas to be assessed and may have specific questions for each domain. In general they are intended for clinical practice and not research purposes. They are often included in texts that address family assessment. They are not reported in the literature but are frequently used for individual family assessment and could be reported as instruments in case studies. The strengths of the assessment guides generally are the comprehensive description of the domains of family functioning that may need to be assessed and examples of open-ended questions to assess specific domains. The limitations include lack of reliability and validity data, little reported use in the literature, and lack of comparability across populations or users. They are particularly helpful to beginning clinicians/students who are developing skill in the clinical assessment of family functioning or to clinicians who wish to develop a systematic and uniform method of collecting family data for their practice.

5

Issues in the Use of Family
Functioning Measures

FAMILY FUNCTIONING MEASUREMENT
AND ANALYSIS ISSUES

Once a preliminary decision is made regarding choice of an instrument to measure family functioning, other important issues need to be addressed. A critical question for clinicians and researchers is: "From whom am I going to collect information and if I collect it from multiple members, what meaning does it have?" Most instruments presented here have been designed to measure an individual's perception of family functioning. Feetham (1991a) proposed that research with families be identified as either "family-related research" or "family research." In "family research" the family unit or system is the unit of analysis. Data can be collected from individuals but need to be analyzed in relationship to other family members' perceptions. In contrast, "family-related research" examines variables of concern to the family such as a family member's reaction to the illness of another family member. It may also be appropriate, based on the research question, to gather individual perceptions from dyads or multiple family members (Uphold & Strickland, 1989). When the research question asks about the average family perception, a family mean may be computed on quantitative instruments (Ferketich & Mercer, 1992). When family differences are being explored, a discrepancy score is appropriate, or when shared perception is the phenomenon of interest, a correlation between individual scores is appropriate.

Nevertheless, each technique has consequences (Davis, 1993). For example, while the additive or average score is the only method of analysis that reflects the collective perception of the family and may yield greater variance than do individual mean scores, combined family scores also may obscure very discrepant individual perceptions of family functioning. Some researchers (Harrigan, 1989) compare mean scores for family members (i.e., parents and children) and if not significantly different may average them to more accurately reflect the collective perception of the family. The researcher can also then be assured of not obscuring divergent scores. Data transformation such as weighted scores is another mechanism to address the appropriate pooling of individual data to represent the family unit. In addition, many multivariate analyses require independence of variables. If multiple members' perceptions of family functioning are used in predicting an outcome, this statistical assumption is violated. Techniques such as Lisrel analysis, where correlation of predictor variables can be encompassed, may be used to combat this problem in analysis where samples are of appropriate size.

Discrepancy scores reflect family disagreement or lack of similar perception. This scoring technique is optimal when variation in family scores is anticipated, for example in families with adolescents or families who have a member experiencing chronic illness (Uphold & Strickland, 1989). This method may have a reduced range and variance when compared to actual scale scores. This decreased variance may decrease the likelihood of obtaining statistical significance or obtaining an R^2 of any magnitude (Davis, 1993). Another choice, correlational analysis, describes the relationship among individuals in a family. When combined with measures of central tendency and dispersion, correlations can give a reasonable picture of the relationship between members of a subsystem in a family. The correlation based on individual's taking the same measures, however, is at risk for increased measurement error (Davis, 1993).

In addition, Feetham, Perkins, and Carroll (1993) recently proposed that when data are collected from multiple family members, the analysis plan is stronger if it includes review of data from multiple standpoints. They recommend exploratory data analysis, such as scatter diagram plots, box plots, stem and leaf displays to examine characteristics of the data. The identification of outliers, unique clustering of the data, or skewed distributions all might influence additional analysis and should be evaluated before carrying out any data summarization for the family as unit.

Finally, Campbell (1987) indicated that the obvious work that needs to be done on existing family measurement instruments should preclude the development of new instruments. It can be argued, however, that work needs to proceed in both areas: instrument refinement and instrument development. Dimensions of interest in family functioning vary by the research or clinical question being raised. Good measurement needs to be based in a clear conceptual schema. The choice of a measurement instrument then becomes a match between the questions being addressed and the dimensions of the instrument. The complexity of families resulting in numerous dimensions of interest has generated multiple measures.

QUALITATIVE METHODS IN FAMILY RESEARCH

In recent studies the sole reliance on quantitative measures has been questioned by some scholars (Deatrick, Faux, & Moore, 1993; Gilgun, Daly, & Handel, 1992). Qualitative methods have generated data which can 1) capture the complexity of families, including the meaning families assign to the experiences; 2) collect data on family as a unit; 4) identify concepts not included in quantitative instruments; and 4) provide evidence for the validity of quantitative instruments. Scholars studying families may find qualitative data critical in explaining how families function in certain situations (Deatrick & Knafl, 1990; Knafl & Deatrick, 1990). Deatrick, Faux, and Moore (1993) conducted an analysis of qualitative research on families' experiences with childhood illness. They identified a number of issues to be addressed when conducting qualitative research with families. Their recommendations included: 1) Overall qualitative approach or paradigmatic orientation needs to be specified; 2) If a conceptual model or sensitizing framework is used it needs to be made explicit; 3) The definition of family needs to be specified; 4) The focus of the research needs to be specified (family-focused or family research); and 5) The influence of the child's developmental stage on the validity of the research method needs to be evaluated.

CONCLUSIONS

Several issues were apparent from the review of the 18 instruments.

1. The measures reviewed have been useful in capturing dimensions of family functioning and their relationship to a variety of outcomes.
2. In spite of the comprehensive review of instruments reported here and the broad range of dimensions critiqued, there may be important nuances of family functioning that are not captured by the instruments reviewed. The potential researcher cannot assume, even if psychometric evidence was established on the population under study, that the unique characteristics of the family will be captured by the instrument. Combined methodologies which include qualitative methods should be strongly considered (Zoeller et al., 1993). A recently developed instrument, The Family Systems Stressor-Strength Inventory (FS^{3}I), may be worth reviewing (Mischke-Berkey & Hanson, 1993).
3. As our society becomes more diverse, instruments that are reliable and valid measures of the family in these populations will be needed. The majority of instruments reviewed here do not have reliability and validity data across cultural groups. The number of instruments that are being translated indicates a move to use instruments with diverse populations. Future work needs to focus on psychometric assessment within a variety of cultural groups (Ferketich, Phillips, & Verran, 1993).
4. Feetham proposes that family research refers to the family as a unit of analysis. Family-related research addresses the perception of individual family members. If the systems proposition that a whole is greater than the

sum of its parts is accurate, then there should be increasing emphasis on the family as the unit of analysis. Most instruments reviewed could be used to address the family as the unit of analysis. For example, Sullivan and Fawcett (1991) proposed that data from the FDM could be combined to generate family profiles. McCubbin (personal communication, 1993) is currently using parents' hardiness scores to classify the family. Mother's and father's hardiness scores were classified as either high or low. Then a four-cell typology was created where families could have parents both in the high category, both in the low category, or father high/mother low or father low/mother high. This family unit data can then be used to evaluate relationships with an outcome variable. Data from self-report instruments reviewed, however, could not be used to generate transactional data. Data collection methods such as the interaction scales reviewed, a Reiss's Q-sort exercise, or the Simulated Family Activity Measure (SIMFAM) would need to be used to generate transactional data (Sullivan & Fawcett, 1991).

5. Potential users need to be aware of the dynamic state of most family functioning measures. Researchers are encouraged to contact the developer(s) of the instrument for the status of current work. Changes are anticipated even in the most well-established instruments.

6. Only a few instruments reviewed had versions appropriate for children under 10. The lack of these instruments negatively impacts on the ability to reflect multiple family members' perceptions of family functioning.

7. Individuals using the instruments presented need to carefully consider the normative data reported. Social changes occur over time. These changes may necessitate updating norms for some of the instruments whose normative structure was established years ago (Wilk, 1991).

8. Many studies reviewed used fairly small samples and did not indicate statistical power. Mengel and Davis (1993) indicate that the lack of attention to the statistical power (or sample size) needed may affect the reader's ability to accurately interpret nonsignificant results.

9. There is a lack of theoretical consistency among instruments reviewed that purport to measure the same constructs. This lack of theoretical consistency makes it difficult to compare data collected by different instruments. Researchers need to closely examine the items in the instrument to ascertain whether they represent the concept they wish to study.

Once a conceptual match is identified, choosing instruments or methods needs to be determined by a critical analysis of the characteristics outlined in this review, such as length of instrument, reading level, scoring, psychometric properties including analysis of the populations on which normative data were established, cost, and cross-cultural relevance. With this careful analysis, nurses can make efficient and effective choices.

References

Abell, T. D., Baker, L. C., Clover, R. D., & Ramsey, C. N. (1991). The effects of family functioning on infant birth weight. *Journal of Family Practice, 32*(1), 37–44.

Adelman, A. M., & Shank, J. C. (1988). The association of psychosocial factors with the resolution of abdominal pain. *Family Medicine, 20*(4), 266–270.

Ahmeduzzaman, M., & Roopnarine, J. L. (1991). Sociodemographic factors, functioning style, social support, and fathers' involvement with preschoolers in African-American intact families. *Journal of Marriage and the Family, 54*, 699–707.

Ardone, R., & D'Atena, P. (1988). Il sisteme familiars nella fase dell'adolescenza: Un contributo di ricerca. *Terapia–Familiare, 28*, 19–36.

Arnold, B. R., & Orozco, S. (1989). Physical disability, acculturation, and family interaction among Mexican Americans. *Journal of Applied Rehabilitation Counseling, 20*(2), 28–32.

Arrington, D. (1991). Thinking systems–seeing systems: An integrative model for systematically oriented art therapy. *Arts in Psychotherapy, 18*, 201–211.

Austin, J. K., & Huberty, T. J. (1989). Revision of the Family APGAR for use by 8-year-olds. *Family Systems Medicine, 7*, 323–327.

Barnhill, L. (1979). Healthy family systems. *Family Relations, 28*, 94–100.

Beach, E. K., Nagy, C., Tucker, D., & Utz, S. (1988). Perceived stressful life events: A factor in recovery after myocardial infarction. *Progress in Cardiovascular Nursing, 3*(4), 153–157.

Beavers, J. S., Blumberg, S., Timken, K. R., & Weiner, M. D. (1965). Communication patterns of mothers of schizophrenics. *Family Process, 4*, 95–104.

Beavers, J. S., Hampson, R. B., Hulgus, Y. F., & Beavers, W. R. (1986). Coping in families with a retarded child. *Family Process, 25*, 365–378.

Beavers, W. R., & Hampson, R. B. (1990). *Successful families: Assessment and intervention*. New York: W. W. Norton.

Beavers, W. R., & Hampson, R. B. (1993). Measuring family competence: The Beavers system model. In F. Walsh (Ed.), *Normal family processes* (2nd ed., pp. 73–95). New York: Guilford.

Beavers, W. R., Hampson, R. B., & Hulgus, Y. F. (1985). The Beavers systems approach to family assessment. *Family Process, 24*, 398–405.

Beavers, W. R., Hampson, R. B., & Hulgus, Y. F. (1990). *Manual: Beavers systems model of family assessment*. Dallas: Southwest Family Institute.

Beavers, W. R., & Voeller, M. N. (1983). Family models: Comparing the Olson circumplex model with the Beavers system model. *Family Process, 22*, 85–98.

Bennett, C. (1992). The incest cycle across generations. *Perspectives in Psychiatric Care, 28*(4), 19–23.

Benter, S. E. (1991). Perceived seriousness of children's surgery and family adaptability and cohesion. *Journal of Child–Adolescent Psychiatric Mental Health Nursing, 4*(4), 137–142.

Berkey, K. M., & Hanson, S. M. (1991). *Pocket guide to family assessment and intervention*. St. Louis: Mosby Year Book.

Bernstein, G. A., & Garfinkel, B. (1988). Pedigrees, functioning, and psychopathology in families of school phobic children. *American Journal of Psychiatry, 145*(1), 70–74.

Bernstein, G. A., Svingen, P. H., & Garfinkel, B. D. (1990). School phobia: Patterns of family functioning. *Journal of American Academy of Child Adolescent Psychiatry, 29*(1), 24–30.

Bishop, D. S. (1981). Family therapy and family medicine. In A. Gurman (Ed.), Research and clinical exchange. *American Journal of Family Therapy, 9*(2), 89–95.

Bishop, D. S., & Archambault, R. (1992, September 17–19). *Family functioning in seriously disturbed adolescents.* Presentation at the Second International Conference on the McMaster Model of Family Functioning, Providence, RI.

Bishop, D. S., Epstein, N. B., Keitner, G. I., Miller, I. W., & Srinivasan, S. V. (1986). Stroke: Morale, family functioning, health status, and functional capacity. *Archives of Physical Medicine and Rehabilitation, 67*, 84–87.

Bishop, D. S., & Miller, I. W. (1988). Traumatic brain injury; Empirical family assessment techniques. *Journal of Head Trauma Rehabilitation, 3*(4), 16–30.

Blackman, M., Pitcher, M., & Rauch, B. (1986). A preliminary outcome study of a community group treatment programme for emotionally disturbed adolescents. *Canadian Journal of Psychiatry, 31*, 112–118.

Bloom, B., & Lipetz, M. (1987). *Revisions on the self-report measure of family functioning* (Tech. Rep. No. 2). Boulder, CO: University of Colorado, Center for Family Studies.

Bloom, B. L. (1985). A factor analysis of self-report measures of family functioning. *Family Process, 24*, 225–239.

Bloom, B. L., & Naar, S. (in press). Self-report measures of family functioning: Extensions of a factorial analysis. *Family Process.*

Blossom, H. J. (1991). The personal genogram: An interview technique for selecting family practice residents. *Family Systems Medicine, 9*, 151–158.

Boyd-Franklin, N. (1989). *Black families in therapy.* New York: Guilford.

Brackbill, Y., White, M., Wilson, M., & Kitch, D. (1990). Family dynamics as predictors of infant disposition. *Infant Mental Health Journal, 11*, 113–124.

Breslau, N. (1990). Does brain dysfunction increase children's vulnerability to environmental stress. *Archives of General Psychiatry, 47*, 15–20.

Brinson, J. A. (1991). A comparison of the family environments of black male and female adolescent alcohol users. *Adolescence, 26*, 877–884.

Browne, G. B., Arpin, K., Corey, P., Fitch, M., & Gafni, A. (1990). Prevalence and correlates of family dysfunction and poor adjustment to chronic illness in specialty clinics. *Journal of Clinical Epidemiology, 43*(4), 373–383.

Butler/Brown Family Research Group. (1992, September). Second International Conference on the McMaster Model of Family Functioning. Providence, RI.

Byles, J., Byrne, C., Boyle, M. H., & Offord, D. R. (1988). Ontario child health study: Reliability and validity of the general functioning subscale of the McMaster Family Assessment Device. *Family Process, 27*, 97–104.

Campbell, D. T., & Fiske, D. W. (1959). Convergent and discriminant validation by the multitrait–multimethod matrix. *Psychological Bulletin, 56*, 81–105.

Campbell, T. L. (1987). *Family's impact on health: A critical review and annotated bibliography.* Washington, DC: U. S. Government Printing Office.

Cardenas, L., Vallbona, C., Baker, S., & Yusin, S. (1987). Adult onset diabetes mellitus: Glycemic control and family function. *American Journal of Medical Science, 293*, 28–33.

Carey, P. J., Oberst, M. T., McCubbin, A., & Hughes, S. H. (1991). Appraisal and caregiving burden in family members caring for patients receiving chemotherapy. *Oncology Nursing Forum, 18*, 1341–1348.

Chan, D. H., Donnan, S. P., Chan, N. F., & Chow, G. (1987). A microcomputer-based computerized medical record system for a general practice teaching clinic. *Journal of Family Practice, 24*, 537–541.

Chau, T. T., Hsiao, T. M., Huang, C. T., & Liu, H. W. (1991). A preliminary study of family APGAR index in Chinese. *Koa Hsiung I Hsueh Ko Hsueh Tsa Chih, 7*, 27–31.

Chung, Y. S. (1990). Analysis of factors affecting family function. *Kanho-Hakhoe-Chi, 20*(1), 5–15.

Clover, R. D., Abell, T., Becker, L. A., Crawford, D., & Ramsey, C. N. (1989). Family functioning and stress as predictors of influenza B infections. *Journal of Family Practice, 28*(5), 535–538.

Coburn, J., & Ganong, L. (1989). Bulimic and non-bulimic college females' perceptions of family adaptability and family cohesion. *Journal of Advanced Nursing, 14*(1), 27–33.

Cohen, J. S., & Westhues, A. (1990). *Well-functioning families for adoptive and foster children*. Toronto: University of Toronto Press.

Cowen, L., Corey, M., Keenan, N., Simmons, R., Arndt, E., & Levison, H. (1985). Family adaptation and psychosocial adjustment to cystic fibrosis in the preschool child. *Social Science Medicine, 20*(6), 553–560.

Crowne, D. P., & Marlowe, D. (1964). *The approval motive: Studies in evaluative dependence*. New York: Wiley.

Cunningham, C. E., Benness, B. B., & Siegel, L. S. (1988). Family functioning, time allocation, and parental depression in the families of normal and ADDH children. *Journal of Clinical Child Psychology, 17*(2), 169–177.

Darkenwald, G. G., & Silvestri, K. (1992). *Analysis and assessment of the Newark Literacy Campaign's Adult Tutorial Reading Program: A report to the Ford Foundation* (Grant No. 915-0298). New York: The Ford Foundation.

Darmsted, N., & Cassell, J. (1983). Counseling the deaf substance abuser (Monograph). *Readings in Deafness*, 40–51.

Davis, L. L. (1993). Family scores revisited: A comparison of three approaches to data aggregation. *Western Journal of Nursing Research, 15*(5), 649–657.

Deatrick, J. A., Faux, S. A., & Moore, C. M. (1993). The contribution of qualitative research to the study of families' experiences with childhood illness in families. In S. L. Feetham, S. B. Meister, J. M. Bell, & C. L. Gilliss (Eds.), *The nursing of families: Theory/research/education/practice*. Newbury Park, CA: Sage Publications.

Deatrick, J., & Knafl, K. (1990). Management behaviors: Day-to-day adjustments to childhood chronic conditions. *Journal of Pediatric Nursing, 5*(1), 15–22.

Dickstein, S., Seifer, R., & Sameroff, A. J. (1992, September 17–19). *Providence family study*. Presentation at the Second International Conference on the McMaster Model of Family Functioning, Providence, RI.

Drory, Y., & Florian, V. (1991). Long-term psychosocial adjustment to coronary artery disease. *Archives of Physical Medicine and Rehabilitation, 72*, 326–331.

Dunkin, J. W., Holzwarth, C., & Stratton, T. (1993). Assessment of rural family hardiness: A foundation for intervention. In S. L. Feetham, S. B. Meister, J. M. Bell, & C. L. Gilliss (Eds.), *The nursing of families: Theory/research/education/ practice*. Newbury Park, CA: Sage Publications.

Dunst, C. J., Trivette, C. M., & Deal, A. G. (1988). *Enabling and empowering families*. Cambridge, MA: Brookline Books.

Dyson, L., Edgar, E., & Crnic, K. (1989). Psychological predictors of adjustment by siblings of developmentally disabled children. *American Journal of Mental Retardation, 94,* 292–302.

Ebell, M. H., & Heaton, C. J. (1988). Development and evaluation of a computer genogram. *Journal of Family Practice, 27,* 536–538.

Edman, S. D., Cole, D. A., & Howard, G. B. (1990). Convergent and discriminant validity of FACES III: Family adaptability and cohesion. *Family Process, 29,* 95–103.

Ellwood, M. S., & Stoberg, A. L. (1991). A preliminary investigation of family systems' influences on individual divorce adjustment. *Journal of Divorce and Remarriage, 15,* 157–174.

Epstein, N. B., Baldwin, L. M., & Bishop, D. S. (1983). The McMaster Family Assessment Device. *Journal of Marital and Family Therapy, 9*(2), 171–180.

Epstein, N. B., Bishop, D. S., & Levin, S. (1978). The McMaster Model of Family Functioning. *Journal of Marriage and Family Counseling, 4,* 19–31.

Epstein, N. B., Levin, S., & Bishop, D. S. (1976). The family as a social unit. *Canadian Family Physician, 22,* 1411–1413.

Epstein, N. B., Rakoff, V., & Sigal, J. J. (1968). *Family categories schema.* Monograph prepared by the Family Research Group of the Department of Psychiatry, Jewish General Hospital, Montreal in collaboration with the McGill University Human Development Study.

Erlanger, M. A. (1990). Using the genogram with the older client. *Journal of Mental Health Counseling, 12,* 321–331.

Evans, R. L., Bishop, D. S., Mattock, A. L., Stranahan, S., & Noonan, C. (1987). Predicting post stroke family function: A continuing dilemma. *Psychological Reports, 60,* 691–695.

Evans, R. L., Halar, E. M., & Bishop, D. S. (1986). Family function as a predictor of stroke outcome. *Archives of Physical Medicine and Rehabilitation, 67,* 691–695.

Failla, S., & Jones, L. C. (1991). Families of children with developmental disabilities: An examination of family hardiness. *Research in Nursing & Health, 14,* 41–50.

Fanslow, J., & Shultz, C. (1991). Use of the Family APGAR in the community setting: A pilot study. *Home Healthcare Nurse, 9,* 54–58.

Faux, S. A., & Ford-Gilboe, M. (1993, November). *Family functioning, family hardiness, and quality of life of families with developmentally disabled adults.* Paper in Symposium presented at the Council of Nurse Researchers, Washington, DC.

Feetham, S. (1991a). Conceptual and methodological issues in research of families. In A. Whall & J. Fawcett (Eds.), *Family theory development in nursing: State of the science and art* (pp. 55–68). Philadelphia: F. A. Davis.

Feetham, S. L. (1991b). *Feetham Family Functioning Survey manual.* Washington, DC: Children's National Medical Center.

Feetham, S. L., & Carroll, R. B. (1988, May). *Further development of reliability and validity of the FFFS.* Paper presented at the International Family Nursing Conference, Calgary, Canada.

Feetham, S. L., Perkins, M., & Carroll, R. (1993). Exploratory analysis: A technique for the analysis of dyadic data in research in families. In S. L. Feetham, S. B. Meister, J. M. Bell, & C. L. Gilliss (Eds.), *The nursing of families: Theory/research/education/practice.* Newbury Park, CA: Sage Publications.

Ferketich, S. L., & Mercer, R. T. (1992). Focus on psychometrics: Aggregating family data. *Research in Nursing & Health, 15,* 313–317.

Ferketich, S., Phillips, L., & Verran, J. (1993). Focus on psychometrics: Development and administration of a survey instrument for cross-cultural research. *Research in Nursing & Health, 16,* 227–230.

Fife, B. L., Huhman, M., & Keck, J. (1986). Development of a clinical assessment scale. *Issues in Comprehensive Pediatric Nursing, 9,* 11–31.

Fitzgerald, E., Speer, J., & Trevor, B. (1988). Reliability and validity of the Family Dynamics Measure. In J. M. Bell, L. M. Wright, M. Leahey, W. Watson, & P. L. Changer (Eds.), *Proceedings of the International Family Nursing Conference* (p. 88). University of Calgary, Calgary, Canada.

Flores, M. T., & Sprenkle, D. H. (1988). Can therapists use FACES III with Mexican-Americans? A preliminary analysis. *Journal of Psychotherapy and the Family, 4,* 239–247.

Foulke, F. G., Reeb, K. G., Graham, A. V., & Zyzanski, S. J. (1988). Family function, respiratory illness, and otitis media in urban black infants. *Family Medicine, 20*(2), 128–132.

Fowler, P. C. (1982). Relationship of family environment and personality characteristics: Canonical analyses of self-attributions. *Journal of Clinical Psychology, 38,* 804–810.

Fowler, P. D. (1981). Maximum likelihood factor structure of the Family Environment Scale. *Journal of Clinical Psychology, 37,* 160–164.

Francis, G., & Munjas, B. (1976). Social–psychologic assessment form. *Manual of Socialpsychologic assessment.* Norwalk, CT: Appleton-Century-Crofts.

Friedemann, M. L. (1991). An instrument to evaluate effectiveness in family functioning. *Western Journal of Nursing Research, 13*(2), 220–241.

Friedemann, M. L. (in press). Evaluation of the congruence model with rehabilitating substance abusers. *International Journal of Nursing Studies.*

Friedman, A. S., Tomko, L. A., & Utada, A. (1991). Client and family characteristics that predict better family therapy outcome for adolescent drug abusers. *Family Dynamics of Addiction Quarterly, 1,* 77–93.

Friedman, H., & Krakauer, S. (1992). Learning to draw and interpret standard and time–line genograms: An experimental comparison. *Journal of Family Psychology, 6,* 77–83.

Friedman, H., Rohrbaugh, M., & Krakauer, S. (1988). The time–line genogram: Highlighting temporal aspects of family relationships. *Family Process, 27,* 293–303.

Friedman, M. M. (1986). *Family nursing: Theory and assessment* (pp. 313–316). Norwalk, CT: Appleton-Century-Crofts.

Fristad, M. A. (1989). A comparison of the McMaster and Circumplex family assessment instruments. *Journal of Marital and Family Therapy, 15*(3), 259–269.

Garfinkel, P. E., Garner, D. M., Rose, J., Darby, P. L., Brandes, J. S., O'Hanlon, J., & Walsh, N. (1983). A comparison of characteristics in the families of patients with anorexia nervosa and normal controls. *Psychological Medicine, 13,* 821–828.

Gerson, R. (1984). *The family recorder: Computer-generated genograms.* Atlanta: Humanware Software.

Gerson, R., & McGoldrick, M. (1985). The computerized genogram. *Primary Care, 12,* 535–545.

Gilgun, J. F., Daly, K., & Handel, G. (Eds.). (1992). *Qualitative methods in family research.* Newbury Park, CA: Sage Publications.

Gilliss, C. L., Highley, B. L., Roberts, B. M., & Martinson, I. M. (1989). *Toward a science of family nursing.* Melana Park, CA: Addison-Wesley.

Gilliss, C., Neuhaus, J. M., & Hauck, W. W. (1990). Improving family functioning after cardiac surgery: A randomized trial. *Heart and Lung, 19,* 648–653.

Green, R. G. (1987). Self-report measure of family competence. *American Journal of Family Therapy, 15*(2), 163–168.

Green, R. G. (1989). Choosing family measurement devices for practice and research: An empirical comparison and validation study of the SFI and FACES III. *Social Service Review, 63,* 304–320.

Green, R. G., Harris, R. N., Forte, J. A., & Robinson, M. A. (1991a). Evaluating FACES III and the Circumplex Model: 2,440 families. *Family Process, 30,* 55–73.

Green, R. G., Harris, R. N., Forte, J. A., & Robinson, M. A. (1991b). The wives data and FACES IV: Making things appear simple. *Family Process, 30,* 79–83.

Green, R. G., Kolevzon, M. S., & Vosler, N. R. (1985). The Beavers–Timberlawn Model of family competence and the Circumplex Model of family adaptability and cohesion: Separate but equal? *Family Process, 24,* 385–398.

Greenberg, J. R., Monson, T., & Gesino, J. (1993). Development of University of Wisconsin Family Assessment Caregiver Scale (UW–FACS): A new measure to assess families caring for a frail elderly member. *Journal of Gerontological Social Work, 29*(3/4), 49–68.

Grotevant, H. D., & Carlson, C. I. (1989). *Family assessment: A guide to methods & measures.* New York: Guilford Press.

Gwythe, R. E., Bentz, E. J., Drossman, D. A., & Berolzheimer, N. (1993). Validity of the Family APGAR in the patient with irritable bowel. *Family Medicine, 25*(1), 21–25.

Hall, E., Wolff, T., White, M. A., & Wilson, M. E. (1993). Family dynamics during the third trimester of pregnancy in Denmark. *International Journal of Nursing Studies, 31*(1), 87–95.

Halvorsen, J. G. (1991). Self-report family assessment instruments: An evaluative review. *Family Practice Research Journal, 11*(1), 21–55.

Hampson, R. B., & Beavers, W. R. (1987). Comparing males' and females' perspective through family self-report. *Psychiatry, 50*(1), 24–30.

Hampson, R. B., & Beavers, W. R. (1993). *Process and outcome in family therapy.* Manuscript submitted for publication.

Hampson, R. B., Beavers, W. R., & Hanks, C. O. (1993). *Cross-model, cross-method comparisons.* Unpublished manuscript.

Hampson, R. B., Beavers, W. R., & Hulgus, Y. F. (1988). Comparing the Beavers and Circumplex models of family functioning. *Family Process, 27,* 85–92.

Hampson, R. B., Beavers, W. R., & Hulgus, Y. F. (1989). Insiders' and outsiders' views of family: The assessment of family competence and style. *Journal of Family Psychology, 3,* 118–136.

Hampson, R. B., Beavers, W. R., & Hulgus, Y. F. (1990). Cross-ethnic family differences: Interactional assessment of white, black, and Mexican-American families. *Journal of Marital and Family Therapy, 16,* 307–319.

Hampson, R. B., Hulgus, Y. F., & Beavers, W. R. (1991). Comparisons of self-report measures of the Beavers System Model and Olson's Circumplex Model. *Journal of Family Psychology, 4,* 326–340.

Hampson, R. B., Hulgus, Y. F., Beavers, W. R., & Beavers, J. (1988). The assessment of competence in families with a retarded child. *Journal of Family Psychology, 2,* 32–53.

Hampson, R. B., Hyman, T. L., & Beavers, W. R. (1994). Age-of-recall on family-of-origin ratings. *Journal of Marital and Family Therapy, 20*(1), 61–67.

Hardy, K. V., & Laszloffy, T. A. (1992). Training racially sensitive family therapists: Context, content, and contact. *Families in Society, 73,* 364–370.

Harrigan, M. P. (1989). Family households comprised of three generations: The relationships of individual, dyadic, and family measures to family functioning (Doctoral dissertation, Virginia Commonwealth University, Richmond, Virginia, 1989). *Dissertation Abstracts International, 50,* 2666.

Hartman, A. (1978). Diagrammatic assessment of family relationships. *Social Casework, 59*, 465–476.

Hauser, S. T., Jacobson, A. M., Lavori, P., Wolfsdorf, J. I., Herskowitz, R. D., Milley, J. E., Bliss, R., Wertliebk, D., & Stein, J. (1990). Adherence among children and adolescents with insulin-dependent diabetes mellitus over a four-year longitudinal follow-up: II Immediate and long-term linkages with the family milieu. *Journal of Pediatric Psychology, 15*, 527–542.

Henggeler, S. W., Burr-Harris, A. W., Borduin, C. M., & McCallum, G. (1991). Use of the Family Adaptability and Cohesion Evaluation Scales in child clinical research. *Journal of Abnormal Child Psychology, 19*(1), 53–63.

Herth, K. A. (1989). The root of it all—Genograms as a nursing assessment tool. *Journal of Gerontological Nursing, 15*(12), 32–37.

Holman, A. M. (1983). *Family assessment: Tools for understanding and intervention.* Beverly Hills: Sage.

Horton, A. D., & Retzlaff, P. D. (1991). Family assessment: Toward DSM-III-R relevancy. *Family Personality, 47*, 94–100.

Howe, K. G. (1990). Daughters discover their mothers through biographies and genograms: Educational and clinical parallels. *Women & Therapy, 10*, 31–40.

Hudson, W. (1982). *The clinical measurement package.* Homewood, IL: The Dorsey Press.

Hulgus, Y. F., & Hampson, R. B. (1986). *Psychometric evaluation of the self report family inventory.* Dallas: Southwest Family Institute.

Hulsey, T. L., Sexton, M. C., & Nash, M. R. (1992). Perceptions of family functioning and the occurrence of childhood sexual abuse. *Bulletin of the Menninger Clinic, 56*, 438–450.

Ingersoll-Dayton, B., & Arndt, B. (1991). Uses of the genogram with the elderly and their families. *Journal of Gerontological Social Work, 15*, 105–120.

Jackson, E. P., Dunham, R. M., & Kidwell, J. S. (1990). The effects of gender and of family cohesion and adaptability on identity status. *Journal of Adolescent Research, 5*, 161–174.

Jacob, T., & Tennenbaum, D. L. (1988). *Family assessment: Rationale, methods, and future directions.* New York: Plenum Press.

Joffe, R. T., Offord, D. R., & Boyle, M. H. (1988). Ontario child health study: Suicidal behavior in youth age 2–16 years. *American Journal of Psychiatry, 145*, 1420–1423.

Kabacoff, R. I., Miller, I. W., Bishop, D. S., Epstein, N. B., & Keitner, G. I. (1990). A psychometric study of the McMaster Family Assessment Device in psychiatric, medical and nonclinical samples. *Journal of Family Psychology, 3*(4), 431–439.

Kang, S., Kleinman, P. H., Todd, T., & Kemp, J. (1991). Familial and individual functioning in a sample of adult cocaine abusers. *Journal of Drug Issues, 21*, 579–592.

Kawash, G., & Kozeluk, L. (1990). Self-esteem in early adolescence as a function of position within Olson's Circumplex Model of marital and family systems. *Social Behavior and Personality, 18*, 189–196.

Keitner, G. I. (Ed.). (1990). *Depression and families: Impact and treatment.* Washington, DC: American Psychiatric Press.

Keitner, G. I., Fodor, J., Ryan, C. E., Miller, I. W., Bishop, D. S., & Epstein, N. B. (1991). A cross-cultural study of major depression and family functioning. *Canadian Journal of Psychiatry, 36*, 254–259.

Keitner, G. I., Miller, I. W., Epstein, N. B., Bishop, D. S., & Fruzzetti, A. E. (1987). Family functioning and the course of major depression. *Comprehensive Psychiatry, 28*, 54–64.

Keitner, G. I., Miller, I. W., Fruzzetti, A. E., Epstein, N. B., Bishop, D. S., & Norman, W. H. (1987). Family functioning and suicidal behavior in psychiatric inpatients with major depression. *Psychiatry, 50*, 242–255.

Keitner, G. I., Ryan, C. E., Fodor, J., Miller, I. W., Epstein, N. B., & Bishop, D. S. (1990). A cross-cultural study of family functioning. *Contemporary Family Therapy, 12* (5), 439–454.

Keitner, G. I., Ryan, C. E., Miller, I. W., & Norman, W. H. (1992). Recovery and major depression: Factors associated with twelve-month outcome. *American Journal of Psychiatry, 149*, 93–99.

Kelley, P. (1992). Healthy stepfamily functioning. *Families in Society, 73*, 579–587.

Kelly, G. D. (1990). The cultural family of origin: A description of a training strategy. *Counselor Education and Supervision, 30*, 77–84.

Kelsey-Smith, M., & Beavers, W. R. (1981). Family assessment: Centripetal and centrifugal family systems. *American Journal of Family Therapy, 9*(4), 3–12.

Kirchler, E. (1988). Marital happiness and interaction in everyday surroundings: A time-sample diary approach for couples. *Journal of Social and Personal Relationships, 5*, 375–382.

Knafl, K. A., & Deatrick, J. A. (1990). Family management style: Concept analysis and development. *Journal of Pediatric Nursing, 5*(1), 4–14.

Knecht, L. D. (1991). Home apnea monitoring: Mothers' mood states, family functioning and support systems. *Public Health Nursing, 8*(3), 154–160.

Knight, G. P., Tein, J. Y., Shell, R., & Roosa, M. (1992). The cross-ethnic equivalence of parenting and family interaction measures among Hispanic and Anglo-American families. *Child Development, 63*(6), 1392–1403.

Kobasa, S. C. (1979). Stressful life events, personality and health: An inquiry into hardiness. *Journal of Personality and Social Psychology, 37*, 1–11.

Kronenberger, W. G., & Thompson, R. J. (1990). Dimensions of family functioning in families with chronically ill children: A higher order factor analysis of the Family Environment Scale. *Journal of Clinical Child Personality, 19*, 380–388.

Kronenberger, W. G., & Thompson, R. J. (1992). Psychological adaptation of mothers of children with spina bifida: Association with dimensions of social relationships. *Journal of Pediatric Psychology, 17*, 1–14.

Kuehl, B. P., Schumm, W. R., Russell, C. S., & Jurich, A. P. (1988). How do subjects interpret items on Olson's Family Adaptability and Cohesion Evaluation Scales (FACES)? *Educational and Psychological Measurement, 48*, 247–253.

Kustner, M., Vicente, C. M., & Cochoy, L. (1991). The effect of family factors on mental retardation in the Cartuja quarter of Granada. *Aten Primaria, 8*, 299–302.

Ladewig, B. H., Jesse, P. O., & Strickland, M. P. (1992). Children held hostage: Mother's depressive affect and perceptions of family psychosocial functioning. *Journal of Family Issues, 13*(1), 65–80.

Langer, M., Czermak, B., & Ringler, M. (1990). Couple relationship, birth preparation and pregnancy outcome: A prospective controlled study. *Journal of Perinatal Medicine, 18*, 201–208.

Lasky, P., Buckwalter, K. C., Whall, W., Lederman, R., Speer, J., McClane, A., King, J. M., & White, M. A. (1985). Developing an instrument for the assessment of family dynamics. *Western Journal of Nursing Research, 7*, 40–57.

Lawton, M. P. (1972). The dimensions of morale. In D. Kent, R. Kastenbaum, & S. Sherwood (Eds.), *Research, planning, and action for the elderly*. New York: Behavioral Publications.

Lawton, M. P. (1975). The Philadelphia Geriatric Center Morale Scale: A revision. *Journal of Gerontology, 30*, 85–89.

Leavitt, M. B. (1990). Family recovery after vascular surgery. *Heart and Lung, 19*, 486–490.

Lehr, R. F., & Fitzsimmons, G. (1991). Adaptability and cohesion: Implications for understanding the violence-prone system. *Journal of Family Violence, 6*, 255–265.

Lewis, J. M., Beavers, W. R., Gossett, J. T., & Phillips, V. A. (1976). *No single thread: Psychological health in family systems.* New York: Brunner/Mazel.

Like, R. C., Rogers, J., & McGoldrick, M. (1988). Reading and interpreting genograms: A systematic approach. *Journal of Family Practice, 26*, 407–412.

Locke, H. J., & Wallace, K. M. (1959). Short marital adjustment and prediction tests: Their reliability and validity. *Marriage and Family Living, 21*, 251–255.

Loveland-Cherry, C. J., & Horan, M. (1993, November). *The Feetham Family Functioning Survey and health outcomes in parents of full term and preterm infants.* Paper in Symposium presented at Council of Nurse Researchers, Washington, DC.

Loveland-Cherry, C. J., Horan, M., Burman, M., Youngblut, J., & Rogers, W. (Eds.). (1993). Scoring family data: An application with families with preterm infants. In S. L. Feetham, S. B. Meister, J. M. Bell, & C. L. Gilliss (Eds.), *The nursing of families: Theory/research/education/practice.* Newbury Park, CA: Sage Publications.

Loveland-Cherry, C. J., Youngblut, J. M., & Leidy, N. W. (1989). A psychometric analysis of the Family Environment Scale. *Nursing Research, 38*, 262–266.

Lundholm, J. K., & Waters, J. E. (1991). Dysfunctional family systems: Relationships to disordered eating behaviors among university women. *Journal of Substance Abuse, 3*, 97–106.

Margalit, M., & Eysenck, S. (1990). Prediction of coherence in adolescence: Gender differences in social skills, personality, and family climate. *Journal of Research in Personality, 24*, 510–521.

Margalit, M., Leyser, Y., Abraham, Y., & Levy-Osin, M. (1988). Social–environmental characteristics and sense of coherence in Kibbutz families with disabled and nondisabled children. *European Journal of Special Needs Education, 3*(2), 87–98.

Martinez, M., Hays, J., & Soloway, K. (1979). Comparative study of delinquent and nondelinquent Mexican American youths. *Psychological Reports, 44*, 215–221.

Masselam, V. S., Marcus, R. F., & Stunkard, C. L. (1990). Parent–adolescent communication, family functioning, and school performance. *Adolescence, 25*, 724–736.

Mathis, R. D., & Tanner, Z. (1991). Cohesion, adaptability, and satisfaction of family systems in later life. *Family Therapy, 18*, 47–60.

Mathis, R. D., & Yingling, L. C. (1990). Divorcing versus intact families on the circumplex model: An exploration of the dimension of cohesion and adaptability. *Family Therapy, 17*, 262–272.

Maziade, M., Caperaa, P., & Laplante, B. (1985). Value of difficult temperament among 7-year-olds in the general population for predicting psychiatric diagnosis at age 12. *American Journal of Psychiatry, 142*, 943–946.

McCain, G. C. (1990). Family functioning 2 to 4 years after preterm birth. *Journal of Pediatric Nursing, 5*(2), 97–104.

McCubbin, H. I., & Thompson, A. I. (Eds.). (1987). Family Hardiness Index. *Family assessment inventories for research and practice.* Madison: University of Wisconsin.

McCubbin, H. I., & Thompson, A. I. (Eds.). (1991). *Family assessment inventories for research and practice* (2nd ed.). Madison: University of Wisconsin.

McCubbin, H. I., Thompson, A., Pirner, P., & McCubbin, M. (1988). *Family types and strengths: A life cycle and ecological perspective.* Edina, MN: Burges International Group.

McCubbin, H., Thompson, A., & Pirner, P. (1986). *Family rituals typologies and family strengths.* Madison Family Coping and Health Project. Madison, WI: University of Wisconsin.

McCubbin, M. A. (1993). Family stress theory and the development of nursing knowledge about family adaptation. In S. L. Feetham, S. B. Meister, J. M. Bell, & C. L. Gilliss (Eds.), *The nursing of families: Theory/research/education/practice.* Newbury Park, CA: Sage Publications.

McCubbin, M. A., & McCubbin, H. I. (1987). Family stress theory and assessment, the T-Double ABCX model of family adjustment and adaptation. In H. I. McCubbin & A. I. Thompson (Eds.), *Family assessment inventories for research and practice* (pp. 2–32). Madison: University of Wisconsin.

McCubbin, M. A., & McCubbin, H. I. (1993). Families coping with illness: The resiliency model of family stress, adjustment and adaptation. In C. Danielson, B. Hamel-Bissell, & P. Winstead-Fry, *Families, health, and illness.* New York: Mosby.

McCubbin, M. A., McCubbin, H. I., & Thompson, A. I. (1987a). Family Hardiness Index. In H. I. McCubbin & A. I. Thompson (Eds.), *Family assessment inventories for research and practice* (pp. 125–130). Madison: University of Wisconsin.

McCubbin, H. I., McCubbin, M. A., & Thompson, A. I. (1987b). FTRI Family Time and Routines Index. In H. I. McCubbin & A. I. Thompson (Eds.), *Family assessment inventories for research and practice* (pp. 137–148). Madison: University of Wisconsin.

McGoldrick, M., Pearce, J. K., & Giordano, J. (Eds.). (1982). *Ethnicity and family therapy.* New York: Guilford Press.

McKay, J. R., Murphy, R. T., Rivinus, T. R., & Maisto, S. A. (1991). Family dysfunction and alcohol and drug use in adolescent psychiatric inpatients. *Journal of American Academy of Child Adolescent Psychiatry, 30*(6), 967–972.

McKelvey, J., Waller, D. A., Stewart, S. M., Kennard, B. D., North, A. J., & Chipman, J. J. (1989). Family support for diabetes: A pilot study for measuring disease-specific behaviors. *CHC, 18,* 37–41.

McLinden, S. E. (1990). Mothers' and fathers' reports of the effects of a young child with special needs on the family. *Journal of Early Intervention, 14,* 249–259.

Mengel, M. (1987). The use of the Family APGAR in screening for family dysfunction in a family practice center. *Journal of Family Practice, 24*(4), 394–398.

Mengel, M. B., Blackett, P. R., Lawler, M. K., Volk, R. J., Viviana, N. J., Stamps, G. S., Dees, M. S., Davis, A. B., & Lovallo, W. L. (1992). Cardiovascular and neuroendocrine responsiveness in diabetic adolescents within a family context: Association with poor diabetic control and dysfunctional family dynamics. *Family Systems Medicine, 10*(1), 5–33.

Mengel, M. B., & Davis, A. B. (1993). The statistical power of family practice research. *Family Practice Research Journal, 13*(2), 105–111.

Mengel, M. B., & Mauksch, L. B. (1989). Disarming the family ghost: A family of origin experience. *Family Medicine, 21,* 45–49.

Mercer, R. T., & Ferketich, S. L. (1990). Predictors of family functioning eight months following birth. *Nursing Research, 39,* 76–82.

Mercer, R. T., Ferketich, S. L., DeJoseph, J., May, K., & Sokkid, D. (1988). Effect of stress on family functioning during pregnancy. *Nursing Research, 37,* 268–275.

Miller, I. W., Bishop, D. S., Keitner, G. I., & Epstein, N. B. (in press). *The McMaster approach to families: Theory, treatment and research.* New York: Pergamon Press.

Miller, I. W., Epstein, N. B., Bishop, D. S., & Keitner, G. I. (1985). The McMaster Family Assessment Device: Reliability and validity. *Journal of Marital and Family Therapy, 11*(4), 345–356.

Miller, I. W., Kabacoff, R. I., Keitner, G. I., Epstein, N. B., & Bishop, D. S. (1986). Family functioning in the families of psychiatric patients. *Comprehensive Psychiatry, 27,* 302–312.

Miller, I. W., & Keitner, G. I. (1992, September 17–19). *Depression treatment study.* Presentation at the Second International Conference on the McMaster Model of Family Functioning, Providence, RI.

Miller, I. W., Keitner, G. I., Whisman, M. A., Ryan, C. E., Epstein, N. B., & Bishop, D. S. (1992). Depressed patients with dysfunctional families: Description and course of illness. *Journal of Abnormal Psychology, 101,* 637–646.

Mischke-Berkey, K., & Hanson, S. M. (1993). *Family Systems Stressor-Strength Inventory (FS³I).* Oregon Health Sciences University, Department of Family Nursing, Portland, OR.

Moos, R. H. (1974). *Family Environment Scale preliminary manual.* Palo Alto, CA: Consulting Psychologists Press.

Moos, R. H. (1990). Conceptual and empirical approaches to developing family-based assessment procedures. Resolving the case of the Family Environmental Scale. *Family Process, 29,* 199–208.

Moos, R. H., & Moos, B. S. (1986). *Family Environment Scale manual (2nd ed.).* Palo Alto, CA: Consulting Psychologists Press.

Morris, T. M. (1990). Culturally sensitive family assessment: An evaluation of the Family Assessment Device used with Hawaiian-American and Japanese-American families. *Family Process, 29,* 105–116.

Munet-Vilaro, F., & Egan, M. (1990). Reliability issues of the Family Environment Scale for cross-cultural research. *Nursing Research, 39,* 244–247.

Munkres, A., Oberst, M. T., & Hughes, S. H. (1992). Appraisal of illness, symptom distress, self care burden, and mood states in patients receiving chemotherapy for initial and recurring cancer. *Oncology Nursing Forum, 19*(8), 1201–1209.

Murdock, M. (Producer), & Beavers, W. R. (Consultant). (1992). *Family assessment videotape series* [Videotape]. Dunmore, PA: W. W. Norton.

Nash, M. R., Hulsey, T. L., Sexton, M. C., Harralson, T. L., & Lambert, W. (1993). Long-term sequelae of childhood sexual abuse: Perceived family environment, psychopathology, and dissociation. *Journal of Consulting and Clinical Psychology, 61,* 276–283.

Nicholson, A. C., Titler, M., Montgomery, L. A., Kleiber, C., Craft, M., Halm, M., Buckwalter, K., & Johnson, S. (1993). Effects of child visitation in adult critical care units: A pilot study. *Heart and Lung, 22,* 36–45.

Noller, P., & Shum, D. (1990). The couple version of FACES III: Validity and reliability. *Journal of Family Psychology, 3,* 440–445.

Novy, D. M., Gaa, J. P., Frankiewicz, R. G., Liverman, D., & Amerikaner, M. (1992). The association between patterns of family functioning and ego development. *Adolescence, 27*(105), 25–35.

Oberst, M. T., Hughes, S. H., Chang, A. S., & McCubbin, M. A. (1991). Self care burden, stress appraisal, and mood among persons receiving radiotherapy. *Cancer Nursing, 14,* 71–78.

Oliver, J. M., Handal, P. J., Enos, D. M., & May, M. J. (1988). Factor structure of the Family Environment Scale: Factors based on items and subscales. *Educational and Psychological Measurement, 48,* 469–477.

Olson, D. H. (1986). Circumplex Model VII: Validation studies and FACES III. *Family Process, 25,* 337–351.

Olson, D. H. (1989). Circumplex Model of Family Systems VIII: Family assessment and intervention. In D. Olson, C. S. Russell, & D. H. Sprenkle. *Circumplex model: Systemic assessment and treatment of families* (pp. 7–49). Binghamton, NY: Haworth Press.

Olson, D. H. (1991). Commentary: Three-dimensional (3-D) Circumplex Model and revised scoring of FACES III. *Family Process, 30,* 74–79.

Olson, D. H., Bell, R., & Portner, J. (1991). *FACES II.* (available from authors).

Olson, D. H., McCubbin, H. I., Barnes, H., Larsen, A., Muxem, M., & Wilson, M. (1983). *Families: What makes them work.* Beverly Hills, CA: Sage.

Olson, D. H., & Portner, J. (1983). Family adaptability and cohesion evaluation scales. In E. E. Filsinger (Ed.), *Marriage and family assessment.* Beverly Hills, CA: Sage.

Olson, D. H., Sprenkle, D. H., & Russell, C.S. (1979). Circumplex models of marital and family systems I. *Family Process, 18,* 3–15.

Olson, D. H., & Tiesel, J. (1991). *FACES II: Linear scoring & interpretation.* (available from authors).

Olson, D., McCubbin, H., Barnes, H., Larsen, A., Muxen, M., & Wilson, M. (1982). *Family inventories: Inventories used in a national survey of families across the family life cycle.* St. Paul: Family Social Science, University of Minnesota.

Patton, W., & Noller, P. (1991). The family and the unemployed adolescent. *Journal of Adolescence, 14,* 343–361.

Penick, N. I., & Jepsen, D. A. (1992). Family functioning and adolescent career development. Special Section: Work and family concerns. *Career Development Quarterly, 40*(3), 208–222.

Perosa, L. M., & Perosa, S. L. (1990a). The use of a bipolar item format for FACES III: A reconsideration. *Journal of Marital and Family Therapy, 16,* 187–199.

Perosa, L. M., & Perosa, S. L. (1990b). Convergent and discriminant validity for family self-report measures. *Educational and Psychological Measurement, 50,* 855–868.

Philichi, L. M. (1989). Family adaptation during a pediatric intensive care hospitalization. *Journal of Pediatric Nursing, 4*(4), 268–276.

Piercy, F. P., Volk, R. J., Trepper, T., & Sprenkle, D. H. (1991). The relationship of family factors to patterns of adolescent substance abuse. *Family Dynamics of Addictions Quarterly, 1,* 41–54.

Porter, L. W. (1962). Job attitudes in management. *Journal of Applied Psychology, 46*(6), 375–385.

Portes, P. R., Howell, S. C., Brown, J. H., Eichenberger, S., & Mas, C. A. (1992). Family function and children's post-divorce adjustment. *American Journal of Orthopsychiatry, 62,* 613–617.

Pratt, D. M., & Hansen, J. C. (1987). A test of the curvilinear hypothesis with FACES II and III. *Journal of Marital and Family Therapy, 13,* 387–392.

Primomo, J., Yates, B. C., & Woods, N. F. (1990). Social support for women during chronic illness: The relationships among sources and types to adjustment. *Research in Nursing & Health, 13,* 153–161.

Protinsky, H., & Shilts, L. (1990). Adolescent substance use and family cohesion. *Family Therapy, 17,* 173–175.

Reeber, B. J. (1992). Evaluating the effects of a family education intervention. *Rehabilitation Nursing, 17,* 332–336.

Reeb, K., Graham, A., Zyzanski, S., & Kitson, G. (1987). Predicting low birthweight and complicated labor in urban black women: A biopsychosocial perspective. *Social Science & Medicine, 25*(12), 1321–1327.

Richards, E. (1989). Self-reports of differentiation of self and marital compatability as related to family functioning in the third and fourth stages of the family life cycle. *Scholarly Inquiry for Nursing Practice: An International Journal, 3,* 163–175.

Roberts, C. S., & Feetham, S. L. (1982). Assessing family functioning across three areas of relationships. *Nursing Research, 31,* 231–235.

Rogers, J., & Cohn, P. (1987). Impact of a screening family genogram on first encounters in primary care. *Family Practice, 4,* 291–301.

Rogers, J., & Durkin, M. (1984). The semi-structured genogram interview. I: Protocol. II: Evaluation. *Family Systems Medicine, 2,* 176–187.

Rogers, J., & Holloway, R. (1990). Completion rate and reliability of self-administered genogram. *Family Practice, 7,* 149–151.

Rogers, J. C., & Rohrbaugh, M. (1991). The SAGE PAGE trial: Do family genograms make a difference? *Journal of the American Board of Family Practice, 4,* 319–326.

Rogers, J. C., Rohrbaugh, M., & McGoldrick, M. (1992). Can experts predict health risk from family genograms? *Family Medicine, 24,* 209–215.

Rohrbaugh, M., Rogers, J. C., & McGoldrick, M. (1992). How do experts read family genograms? *Family Systems Medicine, 10,* 79–89.

Roosa, M. W., & Beals, J. (1990a). Measurement issues in family assessment: The case of the Family Environment Scale. *Family Process, 29,* 191–198.

Roosa, M. W., & Beals, J. (1990b). A final comment on the case of the Family Environment Scale. *Family Process, 29,* 209–211.

Ross, B., & Cobb, K. (1990). *Family nursing: A nursing process approach* (pp. 255–266). Redwood, CA: Addison-Wesley.

Roy, R., & Thomas, M. R. (1989). Nature of marital relations among chronic pain patients. *Contemporary Family Therapy: An International Journal, 11,* 277–285.

Sahaj, D. A., Smith, C. K., Kimmel, K. L., Houseknecht, R. A., Hewes, R. A., Meyer, B. E., Leduc, L. B., & Danforth, A. (1988). A psychosocial description of a select group of infertile couples. *Journal of Family Practice, 27*(4), 393–397.

Salgado de Bernal, C. (1990). The genogram as a training instrument for family therapists. *Revista Latinoamericana de Psicologia, 22,* 385–420.

Sawin, K. J., & Marshall, J. (1992). Developmental competence in adolescents with an acquired disability. *Rehabilitation Nursing Research, 1*(1), 41–50.

Sawin, K. J., & Marshall, J. (1993, February). *The experience of chronic illness from the adolescent and parent perspective.* Paper presented at the annual meeting of the Southern Nursing Research Society, Birmingham, AL.

Sawyer, E. H. (1992). Family functioning when children have cystic fibrosis. *Journal of Pediatric Nursing, 7*(5), 304–311.

Sawyer, M. G., Sarris, A., Baghurst, P. A., Cross, D. G., & Kalucy, R. S. (1988). Family Assessment Device: Reports from mothers, fathers, and adolescents in community and clinic families. *Journal of Marital and Family Therapy, 14*(3), 287–296.

Shapiro, J., Neinstein, L. S., & Rabinovitz, S. (1987). The Family APGAR: Use of a simple family-function screening test with adolescents. *Family Systems Medicine, 5*(2), 220–227.

Shean, G., & Lease, C. (1991). The relationship between interaction patterns and agoraphobic fears among college students. *Journal of Psychology, 125,* 271–278.

Shellenberger, S. (1989). Elderly family members and their caregivers: Characteristics and development of the relationship. *Family Systems Medicine, 7,* 317–322.

Shellenberger, S., Shurden, K. W., & Treadwell, T. W. (1988). Faculty training seminars in family systems. *Family Medicine, 20,* 226–227.

Sheridan, M. J., & Green, R. (1993). Family dynamics and individual characteristics of adult children of alcoholics: An empirical analysis. *Journal of Social Service Research, 17*(1/2), 73–97.

Shulman, S., Fisch, R. O., Zempel, C. E., Gadish, O., & Chang, P. (1991). Children with phenylketonuria: The interface of family and child functioning. *Developmental and Behavioral Pediatrics, 12,* 315–321.

Simmons, R. J., Corey, M., Cowen, L., Keenan, N., Robertson, J., & Levison, H. (1987). Behavioral adjustment of latency age children with cystic fibrosis. *Psychosomatic Medicine, 49*(6), 509–516.

Skinner, H. A. (1987). Self-report instruments for family assessment. In T. Jacob (Ed.), *Family interaction and psychopathology* (pp. 427–452). New York: Plenum.

Skinner, H. A., Santa-Barbara, J., & Steinhauer, P. D. (1981, June 3–5). *The Family Assessment Measure: Development of a self-report instrument.* Symposium presented at the Canadian Psychological Association Annual Meeting, Toronto. In T. Jacob (Ed.), *Family interaction and psychopathology* (pp. 427–452). New York: Plenum.

Skinner, H. A., Steinhauer, P. D., & Santa-Barbara, J. (1983). The Family Assessment Measure. *Canadian Journal of Community Mental Health, 2,* 91–105.

Smilkstein, G. (1978). The Family APGAR: A proposal for a family function test and its use by physicians. *Journal of Family Practice, 6,* 1231–1239.

Smilkstein, G. (1992). *The APGAR questionnaires. Screening for social support: Family, friends and work associates.* Unpublished manuscript. University of California-Davis, School of Medicine, Davis, CA.

Smilkstein, G. (1993). Family APGAR analyzed. *Family Medicine, 25*(5), 293.

Smilkstein, G., Ashworth, C., & Montano, D. (1982). Validity and reliability of the family APGAR as a test of family function. *Journal of Family Practice, 15,* 303–311.

Smilkstein, G., Helsper-Lucas, A., Ashworth, C., Montano, D., & Pagel, M. (1984). Prediction of pregnancy complications: An application of the biopsychosocial model. *Social Science and Medicine, 18,* 315–321.

Smith, C. E., Mayer, L. S., Parkhurst, C., Perkins, S., & Pingleton, S. K. (1991). Adaptation in families with a member requiring mechanical ventilation at home. *Heart and Lung, 20,* 349–356.

Sproul, M. S., & Gallagher, R. M. (1982). The genogram as an aid to crises intervention. *Journal of Family Practice, 14,* 959–960.

Sprusinska, E., & Makowska, Z. (1992). The effect of social support on women's perception of global stress and health status. *Medical Pr, 43,* 403–410.

Stark, K. D., Humphrey, L. L., Cook, K., & Lewis, K. (1990). Perceived family environments of depressed and anxious children: Child's and maternal figure's perspectives. *Journal of Abnormal Child Psychology, 18,* 527–547.

Steiner, H., & Levine, S. (1988). Family environment of adolescents and coping in the hospital. *Psychoneuroendocrinology, 13,* 333–338.

Steinhauer, P. D. (1984). Clinical applications of the process model of family functioning. *Canadian Journal of Psychiatry, 29,* 98–111.

Steinhauer, P. D. (1987). The family as a small group: The process model of family functioning. In T. Jacob (Ed.), *Family interaction and psychopathology* (pp. 67–116). New York: Plenum.

Steinhauer, P. D., Johnston, M., Snowden, M., & Santa-Barbara, J. (1988). The foster care research project: Summary and analysis. *Canadian Journal of Psychiatry, 33*(6), 509–516.

Steinhauer, P. D., Santa-Barbara, J., & Skinner, H. A. (1984). The process model of family functioning. *Canadian Journal of Psychiatry, 29,* 77–88.

Steinhauer, P. D., & Tisdall, G. W. (1984). The integrated use of individual and family psychotherapy. *Canadian Journal of Psychiatry, 29,* 89–97.

Stuifbergen, A. K. (1990). Patterns of functioning in families with a chronically ill parent: An exploratory study. *Research in Nursing & Health, 13,* 35–44.

Sullivan, J., & Fawcett, J. (1991). The measurement of family phenomena. In A. Whall & J. Fawcett (Eds.), *Family theory development in nursing: State of the science and art* (pp. 69–84). Philadelphia: F. A. Davis.

Sweeney, L. B. (1988). Impact on families caring for an infant with apnea. *Issues in Comprehensive Pediatric Nursing, 11,* 1–15.

Tishelman, C., Taube, A., & Sacks, L. (1991). Self-reported symptom distress in cancer patients: Reflections of disease, illness or sickness? *Social Science Medicine, 33*, 1229–1240.

Tómasdóttir, M., Wilson, M., White, M. A., & Ágústsdóttir, T. (1991). Family dynamics and infant temperament in urban Iceland. *Scandinavian Journal of Caring Science, 5*, 211–218.

Tomlinson, B., White, M. A., & Wilson, M. (1990). Family dynamics during pregnancy. *Journal of Advanced Nursing, 15*, 683–688.

Touliatos, J., Perlmutter, B. F., & Strauss, M. A. (Eds.). (1990). *Handbook of family measurement techniques*. Newbury Park, CA: Sage.

Trepper, T. S., & Sprenkle, D. H. (1988). The clinical use of the Circumplex Model in the assessment and treatment of intra-family child sexual abuse. *Journal of Psychotherapy and the Family, 4*, 93–111.

Trivette, C. M., Dunst, C. J., Deal, A. G., Hammer, A. W., & Propst, S. (1990). Assessing family strengths and family functioning style. *Topics in Early Childhood Special Education, 10*, 16–35.

Trute, B. (1990). Child and parent predictors of family adjustment in households containing young developmentally disabled children. *Family Relations, 39*, 292–297.

Tubman, J. G. (1991). A pilot study of family life among school-aged children of problem drinking men: Child, mother and family comparisons. *Family Dynamics of Addiction Quarterly, 1*(4), 10–20.

Turner, S., Sloper, P., Knussen, C., & Cunningham, C. (1991). Factors relation to self-sufficiency in children with Down's syndrome. *Journal of Mental Deficiency Research, 35*, 13–24.

Uphold, C. R., & Strickland, O. L. (1989). Issues related to the unit of analysis in family nursing research. *Western Journal of Nursing Research, 11*(4), 405–417.

Van der Veen, F., Howard, K., & Austria, A. (1970). Stability and equivalence of scores based on three different response formats. *Proceedings of the 78th Annual Convention of the American Psychological Association, 5*, 99–100.

Van der Veen, F., & Olson, R. (1981). *Manual and handbook for the family concept assessment method*. Unpublished manuscript.

Van Ripper, M., Ryff, C., & Pridham, K. (1992). Parental and family well-being in families of children with Down syndrome: A comparative study. *Research in Nursing & Health, 15*, 227–235.

Vega, W. A., Patterson, T., Sallis, J., Nader, P., Atkins, C., & Abramson, I. (1986). Cohesion and adaptability in Mexican-American and Anglo families. *Journal of Marriage and the Family, 48*, 857–867.

Visscher, E. M., & Clore, R. R. (1992). The genogram: A strategy for assessment. *Journal of Pediatric Health Care, 6*(6), 361–367.

Vukov, M. G., & Eljdupovic, G. (1991). The Yugoslavian drug addict's family structure. *International Journal of the Addictions, 26*, 415–422.

Walker, L. S., McLaughlin, F. J., & Greene, J. W. (1988). Functional illness and family functioning: A comparison of healthy and somatocizing adolescents. *Family Process, 27*, 317–385.

Wallander, J. L., Vami, J. W., Babani, L., Banis, H. T., & Wilcon, K. T. (1989). Family resources as resistance factors for psychological maladjustment in chronically ill and handicapped children. *Journal of Pediatric Psychology, 14*, 157–173.

Waller, G., Calam, R., & Slade, P. (1989). Eating disorders and family interaction. *British Journal of Clinical Psychology, 28*, 285–286.

Waller, G., Slade, P., & Calam, R. (1990a). Family adaptability and cohesion: Relation to eating attitudes and disorders. *International Journal of Eating Disorders, 9*, 225–228.

Waller, G., Slade, P., & Calam, R. (1990b). Who knows best? Family interaction and eating disorders. *British Journal of Psychiatry, 156*, 546–550.

Westley, W. A., & Epstein, N. B. (1969). *The silent majority: Families of emotionally healthy college students.* San Francisco: Jossey-Bass.

White, M., & Elander, G. (1992). Translation of an instrument: The US–Nordic family dynamics nursing research project. *Scandinavian Journal of Caring Science, 6*(3), 161–164.

Wilk, J. (1991). Family instrument selection and study fit. *Western Journal of Nursing Research, 13*, 549–553.

Wilson, M., Hall, E. O., & White, M. A. (1994). Family dynamics and infant temperament in Danish families. *Scandinavian Journal of Caring Science, 8*, 9–15.

Woods, N. F., Haberman, M. R., & Packard, N. J. (1993). Demands of illness and individual, dyadic, and family adaptation in chronic illness. *Western Journal of Nursing Research, 15*(1), 10–30.

Woods, N. F., & Lewis, F. M. (1992). Design and measurement challenges in family research. *Western Journal of Nursing Research, 14*, 397–403.

Youngblut, J. M., Loveland-Cherry, C. J., & Horan, M. (1993). Maternal employment, family functioning, and preterm infant development at nine and twelve months. *Research in Nursing & Health, 16*, 33–43.

Youngblut, J. M., Loveland, C. J., & Horan, M. (1991). Maternal employment effects on family and preterm infants at three months. *Nursing Research, 40*, 272–275.

Youngblut, J. M., & Shiao, S. P. (1993). Child and family reactions during and after pediatric ICU hospitalization: A pilot study. *Heart and Lung, 22*, 46–54.

Zacks, E., Green, R. J., & Marrow, J. (1988). Comparing lesbian and heterosexual couples on the Circumplex Model: An initial investigation. *Family Process, 27*, 471–483.

Zarski, J. J., DePompei, R., & Zook, A. (1988). Traumatic head injury: Dimensions of family responsivity. *Journal of Head Trauma Rehabilitation, 3*, 31–41.

Zoeller, L., Knafl, K., Breitmayer, B., & Gallo, A. (1993, November). *The Feetham Family Functioning Survey and narrative data: Creating an alliance of evidence for understanding family response to chronic illness.* Paper in Symposium presented at the Council of Nurse Researchers, Washington, DC.